"The Divine Mentor is one of the best books on Bible study that I've ever read. Wayne Cordeiro describes reading the Bible as a way to sit at the feet of the many characters and heroes of the Bible as they teach you. What a concept. . . . I highly recommend this book, especially if you're interested in finding an easy way to start a dialogue with God."

—**Karen Wolff,** *Christian-Books-for-Women.com*

"Cordeiro convincingly presents the case for being in God's Word on a daily basis to reap a closer walk with God. . . . This well-written book about developing a daily devotional time provides clear discussion and interesting anecdotes that encourage one to start reading the Bible every day."

—*Church Libraries*

"Wayne Cordeiro knows a secret—for real intimacy with God, consistent daily devotions are not optional. In *The Divine Mentor,* he not only explains the need for, and importance of, devotions but also provides a sensible plan based on Scripture reading and journaling."

—*Charisma*

Books by
Wayne Cordeiro
FROM BETHANY HOUSE PUBLISHERS

The Divine Mentor

Leading on Empty

WAYNE
CORDEIRO

— THE —
DIVINE
MENTOR

BETHANYHOUSE
PUBLISHERS

Published by Bethany House Publishers
11400 Hampshire Avenue South
Bloomington, Minnesota 55438

Bethany House Publishers is a division of
Baker Publishing Group, Grand Rapids, Michigan.

Printed in the United States of America

ISBN 978-0-7642-0579-8

In keeping with biblical principles of creation stewardship, Baker Publishing Group advocates the responsible use of our natural resources. As a member of the Green Press Initiative, our company uses recycled paper when possible. The text paper of this book is comprised of 30% post-consumer waste.

green press
INITIATIVE

The Library of Congress has cataloged the hardcover edition as follows:

Cordeiro, Wayne.
    The Divine Mentor : growing your faith as you sit at the feet of the Savior / Wayne Cordeiro.
       p. cm.
    Summary: "Through engaging stories, lessons, and anecdotes, this book helps Christians discover how to begin—or improve on—a lifelong habit of daily devotions, have a new commitment to the Bible and to God"—Provided by publisher.
    ISBN-13: 978-0-7642-0349-7 (hardcover : alk. paper)
    ISBN-10: 0-7642-0349-5 (hardcover : alk. paper)
    1. Spiritual life—Christianity. 2. Bible—Textbooks. I. Title.
    BV4501.3.C6835   2007
    248.4—dc22   2007014179

This book is dedicated to someone
who saved my life: Jeremiah.

In a world where emergent and entrepreneurial leaders are seeking best practices and innovative strategies, there is a call to return to the Word of God as our base camp.

For years I held the tendency to leave the fountain of Living Water and hew for myself cisterns that I filled with contemporary and missional ideas, but they leaked.[1] Jeremiah encouraged me to talk with divine mentors on a daily basis, and that has changed my life radically.

I also commend others who have instilled in me a love for God's Word: Joe Wittwer, Pastor of Life Center in Spokane, Washington, and Dale Coffing of Albuquerque, New Mexico, who encouraged me to put into print this simple system, which, if you will read on, will radically change your life as well.

CONTENTS

Prologue

Smoke billowed on the horizon. Smoke where there should be no smoke—at least, not a towering column like this one.

It couldn't be good.

Terrorists. What else could it be?

As we approached we could see a few flames licking at piles of rubble. Yet where there had been homes, streets, playgrounds, gardens . . . there was nothing at all. Smoke, ruin, ashes. Nothing more.

Shocked into immobility, we could do nothing but gape. Where were the homes? *Where were the women and children?*

We poured over the edge of the embankment—some sliding, some jumping, some running headlong, falling, getting up, and falling again. Each man ran to the area where his home had been, hoping against hope to see someone moving in the wreckage: a beloved face, a form staggering out of the devastation. But there was no one. And no sound but the dry crackle of flames, fanned by a lonely desert wind.

Where were the bodies? We saw none. The terrorists must have kidnapped every woman and child in the village!

We wept without shame. Some cursed; some called out names in their anguish. Muttering among themselves, clusters began to gather, glancing at one another, nodding, fingering their weapons. It was like the moment before a violent thunderstorm, when the air becomes taut and stifling.

That's when he collapsed on his knees and convulsed in agony. It's not as though *his* loved ones had been spared.

We couldn't help but watch. And as he poured out his sorrow, pleading for help and hope and direction, his body language began to change. Tension seemed to drain away from his shoulders. His hands unclenched, and he lifted his head as he prayed. Finally rising again to his feet, he wiped away his tears, squared his shoulders, and spoke with a steady voice.

Say what you will, *something* happened by that rock on the edge of total devastation. In those few moments, he had found strength, confidence, and fresh resolve. God must have given him a plan too, because it wasn't long before we set off like the wind on the trail of the invaders.

In that moment, we could believe again. And rising among us was the confidence that we would recover from the ashes of Ziklag all we had lost . . . and maybe even more.

Introduction

My best friends are in the Bible. Let me introduce you to one of my closest: David.

The two of you have already met? You *did* recognize him, didn't you? You probably know him better as *King David*, but when this incident took place,[1] he still had a long road ahead before he would take the throne of ancient Israel.

And that brings me to something truly remarkable.

David has been gone from this earth for more than three millennia. Yet he and I still meet weekly. He still teaches, he still speaks, he still encourages and trains.

By walking with David amid the smoldering ruins of Ziklag, I find help and strength for challenges that come my own way.

And he's not alone—he's among a choice community of top-flight instructors! Over the years I have sailed with Noah; I have trekked with Moses. Entering the world of the Bible to learn from my friends and heroes *changes* me.

Jeremiah saved my life. Nehemiah buoyed my faltering ministry. Through his struggles with riches and greed, Solomon tutored me to be a person of excellence without opulence.

I have often heard young leaders decrying the scarcity of mentors. But we have been looking in the wrong places, for the greatest mentors will not be found among those currently on earth. They await us from another gallery.

When the student is ready, the mentors will appear. These heroes and legends have been expecting you.

For whatever was written in earlier times was written for our instruction, so that through perseverance and the encouragement of the Scriptures we might have hope.[2]

Encouragement is God's native tongue. But encouragement without change is like a bicycle with only one pedal. Our participation is required. *Encouragement turns into hope when His instructions find our ready acceptance and application.*

The journey on which you're about to embark is interactive. The lessons you will garner in this book have been distilled from more than thirty-three years of friendships with the mentors of the ages. What you're about to learn has been the most important key to everything I have done. It is not a program. It is a lifetime adventure offered only to avid students of life.

We have only one life to live on this spinning globe, and many people are already halfway through before they realize that life will not fall neatly into our laps without our participation and involvement. Or, worse, that life will not remain neat and tidy in the face of our poor choices. Life will only yield its best fruit to diligent farmers and its treasures to industrious pilgrims.

I have spoken with hundreds of men and women in their fifties, sixties, and older who grieve over memories of foolish decisions.

"Oh," they say, "how I wish I knew *then* what I know *now!*" If only they had understood; if only they'd been able to see; if only they'd stepped back to get some perspective—*then*, perhaps, they would have raised their kids differently. Or not destroyed their health. Or not wrecked their marriage. Or they would have avoided a thousand nameless heartbreaks that have placed in them a never-fading regret.

DIVINE MENTORS

You don't have to live with an endless string of if-onlys. You really don't! God has given an assignment to certain men and women who, though dead, "still speak."[3]

These instructors have been delegated the task and obligation to tutor those who enroll. By shadowing these men and women, you can:

- •• Find the help you need when difficult tests come
- •• Walk with both the heroes and the fools of the Bible
- •• Start thinking like God thinks, so you can respond as He responds
- •• Avoid costly errors and so avoid decades of misery.

The mentors will lead you to strength, direction, and hope even when you come to life's narrowest and most frightening passages.

And the Holy Spirit promises to exhale key lessons from the past into your present and make them come alive. Abraham will mentor you on faith. You will learn from Samson about sexual self-control. Daniel will instruct you in how to influence your community. Ruth will teach you about love and loyalty.

Let me take you on the greatest adventure you'll ever experience. Come walk with me as we visit God's men and women of faith (as well as a few scoundrels).

They all await your audience.

THE VOICE
THAT
BRINGS
LIFE

1

Sacred Enclosures

Above all else, guard your heart,
for it is the wellspring of life.[1]
— S O L O M O N

O ne fine summer day in 1606, in a grove of towering Sequoias, in a place that would come to be known as California, a tiny seedling poked up through the virgin soil. Drawing energy from the filtered sunlight of the towering sentinals, the infant lifted its miniature arms to the light and warmth that had awakened it.

A year later, as the seedling turned sapling, the London Company established the Jamestown settlement in Virginia.

A year after that, as the sapling became a young Sequoia, an adventurer named Samuel de Champlain founded Quebec City in New France, a territory that would one day be called Canada.

After three more years, when the Sequoia's top was eleven feet above the forest floor, a group of scholars released an elegant English translation of the Bible that would be known as the *King James Version.*

In 1618, when the tree was nearly two stories high, Europe became embroiled in a conflict that history books would one day call The Thirty Years War.

As the tree continued to grow, America became a nation, fought a civil war, joined Europe in fighting two world wars, put men on the moon, and suffered at the hands of terrorists on September 11, 2001.

Through all of those events, spanning centuries, the seedling became a towering titan of the forest, soaring over 240 feet into the California sunshine.

And then, just a couple of years ago, the tree fell to the earth in a thunderous crash. It was the first of Yosemite's magnificent Sequoias to fall in many years, and the Forest Service authorized an investigation. What mysterious force had slain the giant? What would cause such a majestic tree to fall in this way?

There had been no windstorms, fires, floods, or lightning strikes. The toppled tree showed no evidence of animal or insect damage. As park rangers and forestry experts examined the downed behemoth, they came to a startling conclusion.

Foot traffic.

In an interview with CNN, ranger Deb Schweizer explained that foot traffic around the base of the tree over the years had damaged the root system and contributed to the collapse. She added that park officials had now instituted a policy of fencing some of the oldest, largest, and most historically significant trees, "to keep the public from trampling the root systems of these giants."

After watching that report, I sat back in my chair. As King Solomon related in the book of Proverbs: "When I saw, I reflected upon it; I looked, and received instruction."[2]

I thought, *Even stalwart and venerable trees that have lived for hundreds of years can't survive when there is no protection—no sacred enclosure around their root systems.*

What's true for the Sequoias is also true for you and me. We have delicate root systems—more fragile than we would ever imagine—and unless we find a way to protect and nourish those roots, we too will fall. It may be in one great physical, emotional, or moral collapse, or it may be little by little through months and years, gradually weakening our lives, eroding our personalities, killing the essence of who we are and who we would like to become.

Believe me, I know.

A Friend Who Saved My Life and Ministry

My daily time before the feet of Christ allows the biblical mentors access to me. It brings me face-to-face with others who were discouraged in ministry.

That's where I was. So I made appointments with several men who know my story.

One was Joseph, who, while doing his best for God, was summarily forgotten for two years in prison.

Another was Elijah, who was depressed and despondent.

Furthermore there was David, who after returning from battle, found that his family had been taken captive and all his belongings stolen. It was then that he and his men wept until they could weep no more. Ever felt that way?

But it was Jeremiah who saved my life.

My personal boat had capsized. I had depleted my system until my body's chemistry was exhausted. I had lost my vision and my desire to continue. A low-grade depression enveloped me like a black cloud. I was constantly checking to see if I had enough saved to retire early, run for the border, and be anonymous forever.

Through many months of agony, I pruned as much as I could in order to loosen the noose that was tightening around my heart.

Open to any reasonable job offers, I struggled to continue my preaching schedule and ministry duties. But one thing I never pruned was my daily devotions. I am unspeakably glad. It saved my future.

It was a morning coffee time. I sat with one of my accountability partners: Jeremiah.

He sympathized with me as I poured out my heart to him. We had something in common that day. Seemed he had run into the same wall I hit. And I think I found the same end of the rope that he had. I was treading water in the midst of a storm-tossed ocean. It would only be a matter of time before I let go of hope.

Jeremiah had been ridiculed, disregarded, and ostracized. Jeremiah had been surrounded by hopelessness and unbelief.

> Look, they keep saying to me, "Where is the word of the Lord? Let it come now!"[3]

Jeremiah understood. Jeremiah felt what I felt. I was comforted by his empathy.

I felt so fried and discarded. *Where are God's promised healing and renewal?* I wondered. *If they don't come now, what's the use?* I was thrashing in a sea of despair, and there had been no help in sight.

It was the next verse that saved me. No, it wasn't a magic potion. It was a statement from a friend—gentle but firm. Originally speaking to the Lord, Jeremiah said: *"But as for me, I have not hurried away from being a shepherd after You."*[4]

He said it in a way only a friend could. Rough but not coarse. Straight but not wounding. In so many words:

> You can leave if you want to. But I'm not going to be in a hurry. He called me to be a shepherd. Now, I might be a sick shepherd or a hurting shepherd, but I'm not an *ex*-shepherd. You can do what you want to, but as for me, I'm staying with the program.

Jeremiah threw me a plank in the middle of that raging sea. Not a full lifeboat, mind you, and I wasn't ashore yet. It was just a plank . . . a plank I held on to, a plank that kept me afloat until the rescue boat arrived. I still had to hang on, but it was what I needed.

I guess it was a challenge from one friend to another. Whatever it was, it kept me alive. It saved my ministry. It gave me the strength I couldn't do without.

Jeremiah went through so much more than I did, yet he never denounced my struggle as petty or unimportant. Jeremiah understood as only a friend would. Because I had sat with him many times, I had the relationship I needed to hear his advice, his challenge, his love for struggling shepherds like me.

I wonder: How many people feel weary, fed up, and ready to cash it all in? How many, like me, have allowed heavy foot traffic to damage their roots? When we do, we're in danger of crashing to the ground.

It was a sacred enclosure around my roots that saved me from falling. It was not an absence of stress or of challenge. It was not an absence of problems. It was a sacred enclosure that guarded my foundation and allowed me to keep standing.

What kind of foot traffic do you deal with every day? More than you might imagine.

Some of us suffer the wear and tear of long daily commutes. We find ourselves responding to unending e-mails, phone calls, text messages, and Blackberry bleeps.

Noise. Chatter. Traffic. Crowds. Politics. Talk radio. Telephone. Television. The neighbor's dog. Bills. Worries. Responsibilities. Deadlines. Endless chores. Demanding children. Relational bruises.

Foot traffic wears on us. We can't evade most of it, and that's not really the solution anyway. What we need to do is protect the most important part of us . . . that deep down, soulish part of life that links with our Creator.

I want to challenge you to develop a lifelong habit that will place a sacred enclosure around the roots of your soul. You can't afford to neglect this, for, as David asks, "If the foundations are destroyed, what can the righteous do?"[5]

We need to hear and heed this most important life lesson. And who would know better about the foundations of human life than the Architect and Builder himself?

ONE THING

Jesus tells the story of protecting life's root systems in Luke 10:38–42.

> Now as they were traveling along, He entered a village; and a woman named Martha welcomed Him into her home. She had a sister called Mary, who was seated at the Lord's feet, listening to His word. But Martha was distracted with all her preparations; and she came up to Him and said, "Lord, do You not care that my sister has left me to do all the serving alone? Then tell her to help me." But the Lord answered and said to her, "Martha, Martha, you are worried and bothered about so many things; but only one thing is necessary, for Mary has chosen the good part, which shall not be taken away from her."

Both sisters dearly loved Jesus. Imagine how they scurried about their home to get things ready for His arrival. This wasn't just any generic visitor; both Mary and Martha recognized Jesus as the long-awaited Messiah of Israel and the very Son of God.

Before they knew it, there He was, coming up the walk, stepping through the door, opening His arms to embrace them. At that point, Mary dropped all her activities and preparations, set her stack of dishes on the counter, and took a seat at Jesus' feet, as close as she could get. Household tasks could wait. Dinner could wait. She had eyes only for Him. She had ears only to catch His every word.

Martha, however, saw the job as unfinished, so she kept up her busyness at a fever pitch. She was a veritable whirlwind of multitasking—clattering pots, stirring gravy, baking bread. Her agitation escalated when she saw her idle sister. How could she possibly get it all done alone?

Finally the volcanic frustration erupted. Martha interrupted His teaching with an exasperated, "Lord, doesn't it seem unfair to you that my sister just sits here while I do all the work? Tell her to come and help me."[6]

Luke describes Martha as *distracted* with her preparations, using a word that literally means "pulled about." We've all been there, haven't we? Yanked from one thing to the next to the next, until we begin to feel like a rag doll.

Jesus said to His friend, "Martha, you're bothered about so many things. So worried and distracted." And then He said something truly revolutionary: *"Only a few things are necessary, really only one,* for Mary has chosen the good part, which shall not be taken away from her."[7]

What Mary had chosen—her decision to cultivate her relationship with Jesus, above all else—would *never* be taken from her. Not for the rest of her life. Not for eternity.

A sacred enclosure. It's something you choose.

WATCH OVER YOUR HEART

The choices you make regarding the foundations of your life have eternal implications that go far beyond your life span on earth. As Paul told his young pastor-friend Timothy, "Physical training is good, but training for godliness is much better, promising benefits *in this life and in the life to come."*[8]

We can all criticize poor Martha for becoming flustered in the kitchen while her sister sat listening in the living room. But how are we any different? We are both Martha *and* Mary. There will always be demands vying for our time. There will always be brush fires to douse. Yet inside us there will always be a yearning for time to sit at His feet.

Jesus says that when you boil all of life down to the basics—when you think in terms of time *and* eternity—not much is truly important. In fact, He says only one thing is essential.

Will we choose to spend quiet, reflective time alone with the Lord? Or will we allow life's pressures to work us into a frazzle? Will we build a sacred enclosure around our roots, or will we allow frenzied foot traffic to erode our spiritual roots and send us crashing to the earth?

Mary made her choice, and so must we.

Solomon wrote: "Watch over your heart with all diligence, for from it flow the springs of life."[9] He too exhorted us to build a sacred enclosure around the headwaters of our life. To take care to protect that inner spring that nourishes and propels virtually everything else we will ever do.

Just how do you do this? I promise you: If you will develop a daily self-feeding program from the Bible and allow yourself to be daily, hourly mentored by God's Holy Spirit, your life will undergo an unprecedented change for the better.

Protecting and cultivating your spiritual root system is not a pill to swallow that automatically will bring you health, wealth, and a perfect family. But it will give you wide-open access to an all-wise, all-powerful God who will personally walk with you step by step. You'll embark on an adventure that will introduce you to lifelong mentors who may save your health, your marriage, your ministry, and your future.

If you make Mary's choice, then you will find Mary's reward.

2

You Don't Have What It Takes

Your testimonies also are my delight;
They are my counselors.[1]

I didn't have what it took, and I knew it. But what was I to do?

Stepping into my first senior pastorate at the age of thirty-one, I found myself shepherding a little church in a small town way down on the southernmost Hawaiian island.

I worked and studied as hard as I knew how, and I did my best, but after six months of preaching I felt convinced I'd drained every last message between the Bible's front and back covers. I simply didn't know what else to say. Despite my frustration, I continued to study week after week . . . and kept running into one dead end after another.

I knew that if I didn't get help soon, I would self-destruct.

I tried calling other pastors for help—and maybe a little mentoring—but their own busy schedules refused to accommodate me.

One late afternoon, when the cooling breezes began to blow, I left my office and took a walk through the neighborhood. Approaching a historic building, it dawned on me that this was the old missionary church of one of my ministry heroes.

In 1837, God used a man named Titus Coan to bring a great revival to Hawaii. Coan loved these brown-skinned people so much that within three months of his landing he preached his first sermon—*in Hawaiian!*

The islanders were so impressed with his desire to reach them that they came in droves. The sleepy town of ten thousand swelled to more than twenty-five thousand in the ensuing years as natives moved from far-flung districts of the Big Island to hear Titus Coan preach in their own tongue.

As the missionary neared the end of his life, he wrote an autobiography that contained unedited accounts of his activities and accomplishments. Pastor Titus detailed his mistakes as well as his successes—things he shouldn't have done but did and things he should have done but didn't. He wrote about how God encouraged him—even in the down times—and spoke words of correction when he got off on a wrong track.

His book *Life in Hawaii* carries a copyright date of 1882, and by the time I reached Hilo it had been out of print for many years. In hopes of finding an old copy, I paid a call on the Lyman Museum. To my delight, I found what I'd been hungering for.

"Do you have a copy of *Life in Hawaii* by Titus Coan?" I asked the curator. She looked almost as old as the book itself.

"Yes," she said with a touch of ice in her voice. "And what do you intend to use it for?"

"I just want to read it," I said. "I'm a pastor here, and I've heard it's a really good book."

She looked me up and down, hesitated, then with a sigh told me that the library's lone copy was very old and fragile. Only those with special dispensation could enter "The

Archives," the hallowed vault where she kept the book. No one was allowed to borrow or photocopy *Life in Hawaii.*

Since I desperately wanted to get my hands on it, I agreed to sit through a long, drawn-out orientation on the ins and outs of handling this literary treasure. This ancient guardian of The Archives made me feel as if I were being inducted into a secret society.

MENTORED IN THE ARCHIVES

After pledging my driver's license, my firstborn, and all my worldly goods, I followed her into the venerated vault. *So this was The Archives.* I looked around the musty, dimly lit room and observed shelf upon shelf of rare tomes, each individually wrapped in paper to safeguard its riches. She located my book on the third shelf and with the meticulous care of an archeologist uncovering the Holy Grail, placed it on a massive koa (Hawaiian fine-grained redwood) table.

Her hands trembled as she painstakingly unwrapped it, placing the brown covering aside in a neatly folded pile.

"Now, when you read it," she instructed me, "be very careful how you turn each page."

"Okay, no problem," I replied. (I'd already been through the training.) My hands reached out for the book, and I opened it on the rich, dark wood table. Meanwhile, the curator remained standing behind me. After a stretch of uncomfortable moments, she added:

"By the way, *do not Xerox* this," she admonished, emphasizing each word. "Photocopying would damage the pages. If you must copy anything, you'll have to bring in your own pad of paper and hand copy it with a pen."

"Right," I said, "no photocopying. And may God bless you."

Without another word, she left us alone . . . old Titus Coan and the young Wayne Cordeiro. As we sat together, he conversed with me through the medium of the brittle, yellow pages.

In the following months, I would come to marvel that this veteran pioneer was always available to me. I had questions, he had answers. I needed instruction, he had the experience. I needed fresh courage, and he breathed it into me from across the years.

I repeated this ceremony two or three times each week, and eventually the library's guardian and I became good friends. She knew I'd be coming, so she'd watch for me.

To some people, The Archives might have been nothing more than the back room of a museum. But to me it might as well have been a Starbuck's where Pastor Titus and I had long conversations over lattes. Week after week, like an ancient Hebrew scribe painstakingly copying the Torah, I would copy, word for word, the contents of *Life in Hawaii*. Eventually I filled six yellow legal pads.

What a treasure! It was my handwriting, but his heart. Every page of the original brought to life memorable experiences, unfortunate faux pas, and priceless lessons. Coan would confess some mistake he'd made because he didn't know the culture of the Hawaiian people, and then he'd describe what God taught him and how he resolved never to make the same mistake again.

Like a long-awaited inheritance, gems of wisdom from Titus Coan's life spilled from his marvelous book to fill up my own ministry chest. He became my teacher, an ancient mariner instructing me on how to navigate the seas of service. His silent lessons began to shape and form my thinking and philosophy, allowing me to avoid many of the dangers that await all young voyagers intent on launching into uncharted ministry experiences.

It's almost impossible to convey how precious that book became to me.

Frequently I'd step out of the warm sunshine and gentle trade breezes to sit in that stuffy room with a man I will never meet in this life but who became a dear friend to me. Titus Coan, a front-line kingdom warrior from an age long past, was a patient mentor. He gave me all the time I wanted, gradually training and discipling me, smiling down on a young pastor who wanted to love and serve the Hawaiian people just as he did.

Without exaggeration, I believe he probably saved me twenty-five years of suffering in my ministry. By reading his book—by absorbing the content of each page through the pores of my soul—*I gained his wisdom without having to endure the same experiences that wounded him.*

GARNERING WISDOM

As a young pastor, I had to admit honestly that I didn't have what it took to be a leader and shepherd of God's people. When I began, I may have had the zeal and even the calling. However, the very nature of the job caused me to realize that, left to myself, I couldn't finish the race. I needed help from outside myself, and I found it in the warm counsel of Titus Coan.

Since that time I've come to realize that it's more than young pastors who need help. *None* of us has what it takes when we begin!

And what is it we must garner along the way?

Wisdom.

We do not have the wisdom necessary to be the pastor, mother, father, wife, husband, teacher, or leader this generation so urgently needs. We don't have what it takes to connect all the dots that would enable us to apprehend all the promises God has given to us, potent promises that we can walk into and see fulfilled in our lives. We may have dreams and visions, but we don't have the wisdom necessary to navigate the highs and lows we will most certainly encounter. We might have been offered the privilege of a ministry position, but we don't have the wisdom necessary to become all that role will require of us.

In His grace, God gives you and me a measure of faith to get us going—but it's not all we'll need to finish the race, not even close. *That* we must gather and collect along the way. He designed life like this to keep our hearts teachable and compliant with His heart.

Our shortage of wisdom keeps us seeking Him and prevents us from becoming hardhearted. It keeps us humble, malleable, correctable, changeable, and transformable, so that with each new day we might increasingly reflect His image.

In fact, this step-by-step maturing process is what we usually call "a relationship with Christ." Our relationship with Jesus grows and deepens as a greater and richer wisdom takes root and grows inside of us.

How exactly do we get this kind of wisdom?

We have our pick of two very different instructors.

A CHOICE OF INSTRUCTORS

Life has given us two very effective teachers. Both are top-flight instructors, but neither comes cheap. While both are effective, both require something of us. We have to choose one or the other, and if we choose neither, the second will be chosen for us.

The teachers are *Wisdom* and *Consequences*.

We can learn a great deal from either teacher. I should warn you, however, of the huge difference in their instructional styles. While Wisdom will amaze and delight us with her lessons, Consequences will leave us breathless—and not in a good way. The truth is, Consequences is *by far* the tougher teacher of the two.

For one thing, Consequences' enrollment cost and ongoing tuition are sky-high. Oh, she'll teach us well, all right—but by the time we learn her lessons, her instruction may have cost us years. It may have cost us our marriage, our family, our job, our ministry, perhaps even our life. Consequences has a huge back-end cost.

In your younger years, did you ever think you were Super-man or Wonder Woman . . . and then jump off a fence or dog-house to prove it? Not long ago a friend of mine, reflecting on his childhood, told me how his big brother convinced him he was Superboy. Nothing could hurt him! In fact, to prove it, his older brother challenged him to walk over to a patch of white clover and step barefoot on one of the busy honeybees attend-ing the blossoms.

His brother was very convincing. My friend took his little bare feet over to the clover and trod on a bee. He said he didn't know which hurt the most, the stinger in his foot or the reali-zation that he'd been deceived.

He was vulnerable after all.

Every one of us has learned something from personal expe-rience that has made us a little wiser. But such lessons, lessons learned from Consequences, inflict real suffering and acute pain—and sometimes they're much, much more injurious than a bee sting.

Suppose you run full blast into a wall, and *bang,* you break your nose. What did you learn?

Wall hard, nose soft; wall win, nose lose.

Good! You're wiser now. What's the lesson?

Don't run into walls that don't move right along with you.

Congratulations. You've garnered a pearl of wisdom from a personal experience that included some suffering and pain.

So now you've got your pearl. It's pleasing. It's valuable. But that's just *one* pearl . . . *one* nugget, *one* checker piece, *one* bit of treasure. Becoming the husband or wife or teacher or leader you want to be—the person you were created to be—will require a whole bag full of these gems.

How else will you know how to navigate life's twists and turns? To get where you want to go, you'll need far more wisdom than what you gained from your unfortunate experience with the wall.

The truth is, you don't have enough bones in your body to shatter in order to gain the wisdom you'll need to succeed in these difficult days. To garner the necessary wisdom to be the mom or dad, or employer or employee you want to be . . . you just don't have enough noses to break.

Oh, you'll *learn*, on the path of Consequences.

You'll even learn a few things about God, as the psalmist did:

Before I was afflicted, I went astray,
But now I keep Your word. . . .
It is good for me that I was afflicted,
That I may learn Your statutes.[2]

If, for instance, I could visit everyone who's reading this book right now and learn from them the wisdom they have gained through suffering—*without* breaking my nose or anything else—then wouldn't I be a very rich man? I would have wisdom beyond my years. I would have insight far beyond my experience. Way beyond what I could have compiled on my own.

In fact, I'd have the wisdom of the ages.

That's the classroom Wisdom invites you to enter.

In the School of Wisdom

If Consequences has a back-end price, Wisdom has a front-end price. It requires discipline, obedience, consistency, and above all else, time. Then it gladly pours on you its promised tremendous riches.

Do you want to know the biggest difference between Consequences and Wisdom? Wisdom teaches you the lesson *before* you make the mistake. On the other hand, consequences demand that you make the mistake first. Only then will it teach you the lesson. Wisdom puts up the fence at the *top* of the cliff; Consequences visits you in the hospital when you're in traction . . . after they've scraped you up from the cliff's *bottom*.

Solomon put it like this: "A prudent person foresees danger and takes precautions. The simpleton goes blindly on and suffers the consequences."[3] That, in the proverbial nutshell, is the difference between Wisdom and Consequences.

Why not rather gain wisdom from the experience of others? Let *them* testify to what they have learned. In this way, when you hear how a friend ran full speed into a wall and *bang,* broke his nose and shattered his glasses, you can listen and learn when he says, "Whoa! Wall hard, nose soft; glasses and nose break."

By listening, you save all the optometrist bills and all the broken bones. By learning, one lesson at a time, you gain a little wisdom from his experience, and *you don't have to suffer as he did to learn the same lesson.*

When someone stands behind a podium and testifies about his broken marriage or his shattered life or what he did wrong and how God resolved it, *learn* from that experience. This is why the Bible says, "The testimony of the Lord is sure, making wise the simple."[4]

If you and I refuse to learn, we're just simpletons. Naïve. Gullible. God's Word would even call us fools.

A wise person sees consequences ahead of time and makes a change before he runs into the wall. A foolish person just runs into it. He'll have to experience it for himself before he'll learn. And if that's the way we live, we will not gain the wisdom necessary to run this race-of-our-lives successfully.

If you're going to be the person or the leader you need to be in the twenty-first century, you must find out how to learn from the experiences of others. We urgently need people who have wisdom beyond their lifetime, wisdom beyond their own experiences!

In this book I want to offer you what is perhaps the most simple and most important thing in the world. If you will catch this life principle and put it to work, you will save yourself decades of lost time and wasted resources.

I promise you, *I am not overselling, and I do not exaggerate.*

The essential practice I will describe in the following pages will give you the kind of eyes-wide-open wisdom you need to keep from running into brick walls . . . and show you hidden doors so you can walk right through them.

TWO PAINS

Just as there are two teachers in life, so are there two pains. Both can cause suffering, but one moves you forward while the other sets you back.

The two pains have names. They are *Discipline* and *Regret.*

The apostle Paul spoke of this crucial difference in his second letter to a group of immature Christian friends. His first letter had caused them some real emotional pain, almost as if his words had flayed them wide open.

> Even if I caused you sorrow by my letter, I do not regret it. Though I did regret it—I see that my letter hurt you, but only for a little while—yet now I am happy, not because you were made sorry, but because your sorrow led you to repentance. For you became sorrowful as God intended and so were not harmed in any way by us. Godly sorrow brings repentance that leads to salvation and leaves no regret, but worldly sorrow brings death.[5]

The kind of wisdom the Bible offers us takes discipline to extract; again, discipline can cause some pain. Spending time in the Bible is not always convenient or comfortable, nor does it always yield immediate or obvious benefits. Some days it may feel like a drag. Other days it may seem like the last thing you want to do. On some mornings, taking yourself by the collar and sitting yourself down with an open Bible may feel akin to a cold shower or swimming against a current.

What's the alternative? I would simply remind you: The pain of discipline costs far less than the pain of regret.

It isn't even close.

If the pain of discipline can gain for us the wisdom of others—men and women who had to suffer through a great deal of regret—then isn't the pain of discipline worth it? In 1 Corinthians, Paul recalls the experience of some ancient Hebrews from Moses' day: "[Don't] grumble as some of them did, and were destroyed by the destroyer. Now these things happened to them as an example, and *they were written for our instruction, upon whom the ends of the ages have come.*"[6]

It's as if Paul is saying to his friends, "Look, you appear to be in danger of heading down the same road that destroyed your ancestors. Don't you remember, traveling that way brings regret and death? You have a choice here: Either learn from their pain and get back on the right road, or follow their example and end up as they did."

James says it even more plainly. He tells us that we can get wisdom from two primary sources—and that we don't want it from the first! He speaks initially of a wisdom that comes from below: street wisdom. This wisdom from beneath is "earthly, natural, demonic. For where jealousy and selfish ambition exist, there is disorder and every evil thing."[7] That kind of wisdom will get you nowhere in the long run; it will only bring you oceans of regret.

Instead, choose the alternative: "But the wisdom from above is first pure, then peaceable, gentle, reasonable, full of mercy and good fruits."[8]

If you and I don't put together a package of godly wisdom to chart a course through our current season of life, we will go through the season and come out the other end to find nothing but a brown, barren landscape. It won't be a fruitful season. It may even feel like a waste.

You may not be old enough for this exercise, but some of us can look back on particular decades in our lives and wonder, *What happened to me in those years? What came out of my twenties? What was I thinking during my thirties? Where did I take a wrong turn in my forties?* Since we get only seven or eight decades on this earth, every one is immeasurably precious. You don't want to reach the end of a ten-year stretch and realize you were way off the mark or that you frittered it away.

That won't happen to us . . . *if* we collect the wisdom God offers us in His Word. Armed with His cutting-edge eternal truth, we will start to negotiate life's twists and turns, navigate correctly, and remain on course.

What's It Worth?

I opened this chapter with a story about my ministry hero, Titus Coan, who served in Hawaii in the early nineteenth century. Even though this man lived some one hundred thirty years before I came along, the intervening time simply vanished after I was in his presence awhile.

During his stay on earth and ministry in Hawaii, he was attempting to teach and pastor weak human beings, just as I was. He was seeking to keep his life in balance and keep his walk with God fresh, just as I was. He made some big mistakes, just like I was making big mistakes.

But the point is (and I can't emphasize this enough), I didn't have to repeat *his* mistakes. I didn't have to wade out of the mire of *his* failures. I didn't have to spend the years and the tears learning the lessons that *he* learned.

Why? Because he had gone before me! He warned me away from the hazards I might have easily fallen into without his counsel. Again, he saved me untold years of suffering in my ministry. As I said above, by absorbing his words, I gained his wisdom without having to endure the experiences that wounded him.

In fact, his book was so precious to me that when I left Hilo, the board of Lyman Museum located another copy and gave it to me, complete with a newspaper clipping that highlighted Titus Coan's legacy, as well as his obituary. I remember looking at that gift with tears in my eyes and saying, "How come you waited this long? And what am I going to do with all the yellow pads of paper?"

How much would I have paid for a book like this? I would gladly have paid a thousand dollars.

But speculate with me for a moment. . . .

What if my trip to The Archives yielded not just one but dozens of such books, each offering insightful lessons from the past that could save me years of hurtful consequences? What would *that* be worth? If I could get other great men and women of history to write down for me their mistakes and successes, I'd pay thirty thousand for it, easily. It would be a bargain. A steal!

I would do this because I know it would save me a lifetime of suffering. I could gain the wisdom of the ages, way beyond my own lifetime. That would be worth thirty thousand, no question.

But consider the grace of our God! He took about four hundred of His top people and put their raw, unedited stories into a whole library of books. He gathered sixty-six of these books— books about men and women, kings and slaves, soldiers and prophets, housewives and prostitutes, fishermen and courtiers—and put them into one. The Bible records it all, the good parts as well as the bad.

Why did God pack all of these raw accounts into a library (a *biblos*, or Bible) for all time and eternity?

Because it's for us.

Remember what Paul said in 1 Corinthians 10:11? *"These things . . . were written for our instruction, upon whom the ends of the ages have come."* God had these stories written down so that through them we could gain the wisdom of the ages. We don't have to make the same mistakes that Jacob or Esau or Saul made. *God wrote it all out for us.* In sixty-six books, He offers us the wisdom of the ages.

But you don't have to spend thirty thousand dollars to get it. You don't even have to spend a thousand. You can get it all at your local bookstore for ten dollars or even less.

Just ask them where they keep the Bibles.

LEGACY AND LIFE

Suppose I had found a dog-eared paperback copy of *Life in Hawaii* for a dollar fifty at a used bookstore on some street downtown. Let's say I'd just tossed it into the backseat of my car, intending to flip through it someday. Then let's say it found its way into my home, where I stuffed it into the bottom shelf of my bookcase, along with old road atlases and some back issues of *National Geographic.*

Would the book be any less valuable? Would it contain any less potential to transform my ministry and save me years of wasted energy and grief?

No, of course not. The words would be the same, whether they were in a cheap paperback or a locked vault. The difference would be in the *value* I assigned to that book.

I think it should amaze us—stun us—every day how invaluable is this book we call the Bible! God not only marked out these sixty-six books, He also breathed himself into the whole library and said to us, "If you will read this, I will let you sit with Jacob. I will let you walk through the deserts with Moses— and the same wisdom that I gave to Moses, I will transfer to you . . . if you will only take to heart the words written here."

You can walk with Esau and ask him why he sold his birthright.

You can sit by the fire with David and ask him how he felt

when Absalom turned on him or when Nathan confronted him.

It's all here—the Bible is the greatest Book of wisdom in the entire universe. That's why Psalm 119 declares,

Your commandments make me wiser than my enemies,
    For they are ever mine.
I have more insight than my teachers,
    For Your testimonies are my meditation.[9]

The men and women the Lord highlights in His Book continue to bear divine testimony all through the ages. They say to you and me, "This is what I did wrong. This is where I made a false turn. This is where I did better. This is where I pleased the loving heart of my Almighty Father."

Take those life-giving insights and secure them in your heart! You don't need to break your nose and crush your dreams and destroy your future, even though some of the biblical men and women did. You can use the example they display to you and the counsel they offer you to find a better path for you and your loved ones.

The men and women of God's Word have left you with a legacy of life skills; this legacy is yours for the taking. Remember how I haunted the back room of that Hilo museum day after day, spending untold hours copying and pondering the experiences and insights of Titus Coan? I paid a price as a young man to gain that good man's wisdom. Oh, but how could I ever assign a value to what I *received*! It has shaped the rest of my life and ministry to this very day.

Nevertheless, as helpful as Coan's memoirs might have been to me, they can't begin to compare with the mighty insights of God's eternal Word. You and I need to go to the Book and pursue these living truths with all our hearts.

If you are willing, the Bible will give you wisdom beyond your years. It will save you from heartache beyond your imagination.

3

The Self-Feeding
Program

Your words were found and I ate them,
and Your words became for me a joy and
the delight of my heart; for I have been
called by Your name, O Lord God of hosts.[1]

The sullen staff member entered my office, saying only, "I think my season is up here."

I'd heard those words before from others. Over many years as a pastor I've welcomed people in and I've bid them adieu. For some it was a normal part of growing and maturing, but this one would leave me confused. He had been with us four years. "Is there any reason why you feel your time may be up?" I asked.

"Well . . ." he hesitated, "I'm just not being fed here."

I hate those words. Not because I'm insecure, but more because the very culture of New Hope, our church community, is designed to alleviate symptoms like these. For the past ten years, we have intentionally built a culture that includes a self-feeding program for each individual, beginning with our staff.

The refusal of this responsibility opens the floodgates for a codependency of sorts—one that requires others to don the responsibilities God intends for every person.

I challenged him with this picture:

> Imagine that my wife sees me one day, gaunt and emaciated. My eyes are sunken into gray sockets; my body is frail, exposing my skeleton; my abdomen is distended from starvation. I've obviously not been eating. When she sees me in this condition, she exclaims, "What in the world is happening to you?!"
>
> My answer is: "I'm not getting fed around here." Then, continuing my lament: "No one is feeding me."
>
> What do you think her response would be?
>
> *"Feed yourself!"*

I then asked the staff member if he was doing his daily devotions. My words were met with an empty stare. I knew he had let this one life essential drop off his list of what was important to ministry success.

I accepted his resignation.

I remember a time when I was in that exact same place, faced with the looming consequences of a nonexistent self-feeding program. I also recall having delegated that responsibility to others.

THE REALIZATION

Shortly after I became a Christian, I found myself complaining to God about the quality of my church's academic-style preacher who often flew things at a high altitude where I was unable to cruise. I began my complaint in the bathroom after a service.

"God!" I called out, hoping I was alone in the men's room. "I'm going to starve in this place! I'm not getting fed. I'm *dying* here, suffering from malnutrition!"

I'm not sure if it was a chuckle from the stall next to me or a reply from heaven, but I recall becoming acutely conscious of something as the Spirit spoke to me from the depths of my own anguished being.

What about ME? He seemed to whisper. *Am I not enough? Why are you blaming others for your lack of growth? You are depending on once-a-week feedings, but as you grow up you must learn to feed yourself! I will be your Mentor.*

My problem wasn't a lack of resources; my problem was that I was expecting others to spoon-feed me. Until that point I'd resisted God's best programs and His most gifted teacher, the Holy Spirit. He had been inviting me to be His student, but I'd remained unresponsive. I wanted others to do what only I could do: take responsibility for my own spiritual health and nourishment.

As I began to get into the Bible on my own, I saw that Psalm 32:8–9 struck at the core of my error:

> I will instruct you and teach you in the way which you should go; I will counsel you with My eye upon you. Do not be as the horse or as the mule which have no understanding, whose trappings include bit and bridle to hold them in check, otherwise they will not come near to you.

I had to admit the ugly truth: *I* was that horse. *I* was that mule. It's no fun making such a confession. It was time for me to take responsibility for my own future.

THE LAST FIVE PERCENT

I hate to break the bad news to you, but about 80 percent of all you do, anyone can do! For example, going to work, attending meetings, checking e-mail, answering phones, going to soccer games and lunches and dinners.

Additionally, about 15 percent of all you do someone with some measure of training could do in your place. Whether it's selling a product, running a program, teaching a class, or fixing a problem, there is education and training available for someone else to do what you do.

But at least *5 percent of what you do, only you can do*. No one else can do it for you.

Only I can be a husband to my wife, Anna. Only I can be a dad to my three children. Only I can keep my body healthy. And only I can grow spiritually! No one else can do the last 5 percent for me. I alone am responsible for it. *Only you can keep yourself spiritually healthy by feeding yourself. No one can do it for you by proxy.*

It's for this last 5 percent that each of us will be held accountable in that great and final day. It's the last 5 percent that will determine the depth of influence we will have on the generations after us. It's the last 5 percent that will decide how joyful our marriage will be and how genuine our legacy is.

And one of the most important aspects of the 5 percent is this: No one but you can sit before the Lord to hear His instructions for you! Jesus' words again ring true as He speaks to you and me: "Martha, Martha, you are worried and bothered about so many things; but *only one thing is necessary,* for Mary has chosen the good part, which shall not be taken away from her."[2]

The last 5 percent . . . it's something we have to discover and then be responsible for.

- •• Only I can be a husband/wife to my spouse.
- •• Only I can be a father/mother to my children.
- •• Only I can grow myself spiritually.
- •• Only I can keep myself healthy.
- •• Only I can keep myself disciplined.

I know I will need some help with these. I need coaching •

and mentoring. My big challenge still lies before me: *applying what I learn.*

Just as only one thing really is necessary, there's only one place to find this help. Let me introduce you to Someone who has been given the assignment to assure our foundations . . . if we will allow Him.

TRUTH NEEDS A GUIDE

As a new believer I made a very common error. I wanted others to study hard and prepare well so they could dump bushels of knowledge into my brain.

I didn't realize that knowledge—even biblical knowledge—is like sodium in raw form. Sodium can be destructive to humans . . . until it gets converted into a higher form: sodium chloride, or table salt. In the same way, knowledge is never an end in itself. It must be converted into a higher form—wisdom—for it to become useful and beneficial to us. To that end, God sends us the Holy Spirit, who will "guide us into all truth" . . . because *truth needs a guide.*

> I will ask the Father, and He will give you another Helper, that He may be with you forever; that is the Spirit of truth.[3]
> But when He, the Spirit of truth, comes, He will guide you into all the truth.[4]

God has assigned His Spirit to be our Guide—the Guide who will deposit God's very wisdom into our lives.

So how does this work? Does the Divine Mentor implant information and insight into our subconscious minds while we sleep? Does He build a golden aqueduct between heaven and our soul, and then open wisdom's floodgates so that it can pour directly into our minds?

Not exactly.

We receive direct revelation about God and discover His wonderful promises in only one place: the Bible. The psalmist cried out to the Lord, "You have exalted above all things your name and your word."[5]

God's Word, the Bible, is crucially important to our everyday lives. And don't think obscure religious knowledge here. *Think food. Think water. Think air.*

As a pastor who has worked with people for over thirty-three years, let me speak plainly: You won't survive without God's insights and wisdom.

I've encountered many people who believe otherwise, and I've watched them implode. We gain all-important wisdom only as the Divine Mentor instructs us through a living interaction with and understanding of God's Word.

Our need for such a guide becomes increasingly vital as we get closer and closer to the end of history, for that is when spiritual deception will become most rampant.

Paul warned his young disciple Timothy of a startling fact about living in the end times: There would be more false prophets than true ones! He cautioned that many people living in those days will have a strong tendency to be "always learning and never able to come to the knowledge of the truth."[6]

Without the Guide, we can learn facts all day long and yet never move one inch closer to the truth that will make a difference in our lives. But with the Spirit imparting to us God's wisdom as He reveals it to us from His Word, the whole picture changes. With the Lord as our Divine Mentor, the wisdom of the ages gradually becomes our own.

TRAVELING COMPANIONS

Did you know that top athletes always rely on a coach? In terms of "equipment," every superstar performer brings along more than clubs or rackets or cleats.

I've heard people ask, "Why would they need a coach? They're the best in the world!"

That's *why* they're the best in the world. They cannot become and remain the best at what they do until they understand and apply the crucial essential of being coachable.

This is equally true for each of us, so God designated and assigned some of history's best mentors to us. Sometimes they will keep us improving. Other times they will just keep us alive.

> By faith Abel offered to God a better sacrifice than Cain . . .
> and through faith, though he is dead, he still speaks.[7]

Abel *speaks*? This man goes all the way back to when man could still see angels with flaming swords barring the way to the garden of Eden. He called Adam "Dad" and Eve "Mom." He was the first man to ever die on planet earth.

Abel goes back just a bit, don't you think?

Yet the Bible says this man still has something to say to you and me. He will take his place as an assigned mentor. And so will Noah, Abraham, Jacob, Joseph, Elijah, Nahum, John, and Peter. Likewise, Sarah, Deborah, Ruth, Naomi, Mary, Martha, Dorcas, and Priscilla. And scores of others. These men and women, though they no longer maintain an earthly address, wait to speak to you out of the living Word of God.

They are waiting to mentor you—to encourage and correct you—just as a good coach will instruct his players. At times they will raise their voices, because they see you rushing toward a dead end. On other occasions they will stand in your path, like the angel with the drawn sword who blocked Balaam, and say, "You're not going to do it."

When you want to take a left turn down a blind alley or head the wrong direction on a one-way street, it may be Jeremiah or Ezekiel or David who will exhort or reprove you. Regardless, these are phenomenal mentors to have on your side!

I remember grumbling on the golf course one day about how terrible my round was going. (God always seems to answer my prayers, except on the links.) We were playing in a foursome, but I didn't realize a fifth had joined us on the fourteenth green. Just as my grumblings were increasing in decibels, I heard James whisper, "Let the brother of humble circumstances glory in his high position."[8] In other words, "It could be worse!"

Immediately I recognized the voice of someone I had just talked with that morning over coffee. I remember chuckling quietly and whispering to myself, "Busted!"

A Multitude of Mentors

Over a period of about fifteen hundred years, God chose more than forty different men to write down His divine words in a book. Just like He gave the angels assignments to be ministering spirits, so He's given the people of His book the assignment to mentor you and me.

I can't think of a better mentor for a businessman than Solomon, who reached an unbelievable pinnacle of success while still a young man.

I can't think of a better mentor for a pastor than Moses. This great leader shepherded a congregation, not of thousands but of millions! We can walk with him through the desert and feel the sand's heat on our toes.

I can't think of a better mentor for a professional than Luke, the physician, or for an educator than Paul, or for a mother than Mary. You get the idea. God has given these men and women the assignment to mentor His children in every facet of life. They live in the Scriptures by His power and breath, through His inspired Word.

All these have gone before us, Scripture says. And now they're in the grandstands, cheering us on. Isaiah, Sarah, Ezekiel, Mary, Matthew, Ruth, Daniel, Esther—all of them and many more stand ready and eager to mentor us.

We have only to ask.

THE GOOD AND THE BAD: LESSONS FROM BOTH SIDES

There are two basic kinds of mentors in the Bible. Most of them, like Abraham, Daniel, and James, are godly mentors. They teach us how to live wisely, how to please the heart of Almighty God.

But the Bible also features many mentors who, through their examples of foolish or even evil living, teach us how *not* to live. God includes the stories of Cain, Esau, Ahab, Jezebel, Herod, and Judas, allowing their shrill voices to live on so that we do not make the same destructive choices they made. They provide potent illustrations that will speak to us from the downside of poor decisions. Solomon reminds us of this:

> I passed by the field of the sluggard
> And by the vineyard of the man lacking sense,
> And behold, it was completely overgrown with thistles;
> Its surface was covered with nettles,
> And its stone wall was broken down.
> When I saw, I reflected upon it;
> I looked, and *received instruction.*[9]

A few years ago a young man left Hawaii for a short time to enter a popular mission's school of biblical studies. When he returned I asked him, "How were your classes?"

He replied, "Some were dynamite! But some were a total *waste.*"

"What do you mean?"

"Some of the instructors were good, but the rest were awfully bad. So I didn't learn much from them."

"No!" I challenged. "Don't do that! You can learn as much from the bad as the good."

"You don't understand," he said, explaining his plight.

"Some were so tedious, we were bored stiff within three minutes."

"That's fantastic!"

"*What?*"

"You can learn valuable lessons from them," I said. "Take notes on that. Let them read like this: 'Our morning teacher is able to bore us to sleep in only three minutes. This has rarely been accomplished! This must be a miracle.'"

I continued. "*Analyze* what he did: What made it so boring? Was it his monotone voice? Lack of research? Tired passion? If you can figure out how to learn from the bad as well as from the good, you'll learn twice as much in life."

That's why God put into the Bible raw, unedited accounts of men and women behaving both wisely and foolishly. He handpicked these people to mentor us, the good and the bad together. Remember what Paul said? " For everything that was written in the past was written to teach us, so that through endurance and the encouragement of the Scriptures we might have hope."[10]

Lessons come from every angle. So get ready! The best gems will come from those ignoble characters who have left them behind . . . unclaimed. If you will go there, those treasures will belong to you!

Do you want your inheritance? Talking about our standing in Christ, as heirs of God's promise to Abraham, Paul wrote: "As long as the heir is a child, he does not differ at all from a slave although he is owner of everything, but he is under guardians and managers until the date set by the father."[11]

Your inheritance is what God has in store for you, that latent treasure, that potentiality, those possibilities for your life. He keeps most of it under the guardianship of caretakers until you come of age. It's almost as if the biblical mentors are caretakers who steward your inheritance until you come of age. So they will teach you, advise you, tutor you—mentor you—until you receive the fullness of what God intends for you.

You have a divine inheritance waiting. This is held in abeyance, in trust, until you come to a point of maturity. So here's the real question: How badly and how soon do you want your inheritance?

PURSUE THE BEST

The people around you *are* going to influence your life. The influences will be good or bad . . . so pursue the best ones. Don't leave this to chance. Go after it!

> He who walks with wise men will be wise,
> But the companion of fools will suffer harm.[12]

Do you hear your mentor's instructions? We become like those people we hang around with. As far as the "why," you've probably heard the answer so often it sounds like a cliché. But it happens to be the truth. *Wisdom is contagious. It's something you catch more than something you comprehend.*

If we want to be wise, we have to hang around wise men and women. You and I must diligently pursue those who will have the best and most uplifting influence on our lives.

"That's fine," you may be saying, "but I don't have people like that in my life right now. In fact, many people I'm around in my family and at my job aren't living the sort of life I want at all. Where do I find these wise men and women?"

Actually, they're in close proximity—right this moment. They are Joseph, Daniel, Abigail, Isaac, Mary, Jacob, Ruth, Joshua, Esther, Josiah . . . the wisest people in history are waiting for you! When you hang out with them, their insights and perspective on life will rub off on you.

It doesn't matter what age you are, what school you attend, what environment surrounds you—you can choose to be in the company of wise people. And you can start today.

Their voices continue to echo off the hallways of God's house, and after thousands of years not one decibel has been lost through degeneration of sound. Their words are as alive today as the day they were first uttered.

Captured in a kind of time warp, these mentors steward potent lessons of life and wisdom, awaiting a diligent discoverer. The prophets still speak. The coaches still live. The guides await your visit. In fact, they *covet* your friendship and they *expect* your company. Listen to the writer of Hebrews, talking about the Bible's men and women: "And all these . . . did not receive what was promised, because God had provided something better for us, *so that apart from us, they would not be made perfect.*"[13]

Physical death did not terminate their lives. God gave them the eternal assignment to tutor future generations of His children. They received a divine commission to mature us. Apart from us, they wouldn't be complete. They would have lived unfinished lives, because they are made complete only in us.

Discover these mentors as I have! I have oft strolled with David and listened to the sound of his harp in the hills. I have traversed the hot sands of the Sinai with Moses and listened to the Niagara of grumbling skeptics. I frequently have accompanied Solomon and listened to Wisdom shouting in the city square. I have even wrestled with Samson, begging for the answers to why he was so duped by Delilah.

These are real heroes who inspire us through their successes and disciple us through their scars. We will walk alongside their rough, unedited lives, without pretense and with no best-foot-forward performances.

They invite us to enter their dwellings. Are you with me? Our mentors are calling for us.

They've made their decision. The next one is ours.

4

A Place of Refreshment

O taste and see that the Lord is good;
How blessed is the man who takes refuge in Him![1]

Andrew came in angry. His face was flushed red. I'd been conversing with Dan, my administrator, when Andrew burst through the door and slumped into a chair across from me.

"I am really struggling," he moaned. "Do you realize how many hours I've put in these last few weeks?"

He was one of our interns. He was as exuberant as he was new until his excitement for ministry faded with late-night pizzas and early morning setups.

"I don't even have a social life! I'll probably never get married. I can't keep going like this. I have to get out of the ministry."

Dan spoke first, in grandfather-like tones that never sounded condescending. Sensing something deeper than an extensive schedule of activities—like a doctor applying pressure on various areas and asking, "Does this hurt?"—Dan pressed

Andrew in an area that made him uncomfortable.

"Andrew, have you been doing your devotions?"

"What in the world does that have to do with this?" Andrew replied, exasperated and defensive. "I don't have any time for devotions. I'm always too busy. I'm on a dead-end run."

I weighed in. "Andrew, why don't you take the next two weeks and commit to one thing. Don't come in till ten each morning. Take the first two hours and do your devotions. Make them rich and meaningful. We will pay you to spend that time with God, one on one. Then I promise, after two weeks, if you still want out, I will give you a nice severance and my blessing."

That wasn't the answer he was looking for. Maybe he would have been more into sympathy and a week's paid vacation, but that would have missed the target.

"Now go. Start right away," I prompted. (I've discovered that whenever you need to change something, always start small, but start *now*.)

Andrew reluctantly took our advice and left.

Two weeks later, I saw him setting up some chairs for a gathering.

"Well, Andrew, do you still want to leave the ministry?"

"Leave the ministry?" he quipped. "Ministry is my life. There's nothing like it!"

"Ah," I said. "You've been doing your devotions!"

KEEPING WISDOM FRESH

This life essential isn't a cure-all for every problem you'll face, but one thing's for sure: Neglecting devotions will cause you more problems, more quickly, than just about anything you can name. Spending unrushed time alone with God in His Word releases a fountain of refreshment from the very core of your being.

The Bible calls Solomon the wisest man who ever lived. When you read the account of his early years on the throne, you see example after shining example of how divine wisdom enriched his life and his nation.

You hear his prayer for wisdom—not for gold or fame or political power—and you feel in awe.

You consider his first ruling in an extraordinarily difficult case, and you shake your head in wonder.

You consider his efficient organization of government, his far-reaching studies in botany and zoology, and you can understand why the Bible says, "God gave Solomon wisdom and very great insight, and a breadth of understanding as measureless as the sand on the seashore."[2]

And yet . . . if you know Solomon's whole story, you know that in the end he wound up a colossal failure. Why? *How did it happen?* How could he go from being the wisest man who ever lived to one of the Bible's most shocking failures?

Apparently, Solomon forgot where his wisdom came from.

At some point in his career, Solomon stopped drawing from the bottomless well in favor of depending upon his own. The man who defined wisdom for multiplied generations became a fool. In his stunning folly, he planted the seeds for a disastrous civil war that spawned the downfall of his entire people.

It should have never come to this.

Solomon's decline began as soon as he ceased his daily treks to God's well of wisdom—a lesson he himself had recorded in his earlier years: "The fear of the Lord is the beginning of wisdom."[3] What happens when someone forgets or rejects the beginning of wisdom? All the rest of his wisdom collapses in on itself, like a house of cards in a stiff windstorm. Solomon became no longer teachable.

A poor yet wise lad is better than an old and foolish king who no longer knows how to receive instruction.[4]

Solomon ought to be the ultimate reminder that it doesn't matter how smart you are, how much you know, or how many degrees trail your name. If you shun God's counsel and turn away from the mentors He has provided, you're in trouble. It may not be immediately apparent—but in the end, it will be all too obvious to everyone.

THE WORD WILL KEEP YOU PREPARED

The Holy Spirit knows all about the looming gray clouds that will descend on you *next month*. You don't, of course. But He does, and He will prepare you for what's just over the horizon. As you receive His wisdom, you deposit it into the archives of your heart, and it will bear fruit at exactly the right time.

In Matthew 13, Jesus tells a story we usually call the parable of the sower. When the disciples later ask Him to interpret, He explains that the sower's seed represents the Word of God. When He plants a seed of His Word in you, it doesn't necessarily come to fruition today. Fruit can and will be harvested down the road.

How often I've been doing devotions on a particular passage and wondered, *Why am I reading this? It has nothing to do with me.* But remember, that seed takes time to germinate and grow. Could it be that God wants to plant a particular seed in you today because He knows that in a few weeks or months you're going to need the crop of wisdom that will come from it?

This deliberate training of our minds is much like the training of an athlete. When you're in a race, where do you get the strength to run it? In the middle of the contest? Hardly! You got it weeks and months ago, when you were pounding the pavement day after day, paying the price to be in top shape.

It's the strength of months and years and even a lifetime of practice that allows a world-class musician like Yo-Yo Ma to play as he does. He didn't get his expertise yesterday. And he didn't wake up with it this morning. He built up and developed

layer after layer of excellence over years and years of investment. Now, today, he performs so naturally and with such
genius because of his hard work and discipline.

The same is true of our spiritual lives. You will be facing
some very significant decisions in your near future. I don't
know what they are, and neither do you. But the Spirit does,
and His assignment is to bring you the wisdom and the grace
necessary to succeed.

THE WORD WILL KEEP YOU FRUITFUL

It's interesting to see what people will grasp in the hope of
achieving fruitfulness, whether in their love life, business, or
finances. Some use chain letters, some use horoscopes, some
use a porcelain cat or a rabbit's foot. Here's a letter from years
ago that my daughter's friends passed around in junior high:

> *Once you touch this letter, you must keep it. This is a love test.
> It started in 1877. You must keep it, copy it, word for word, and
> give it to five people (not boys!) within five days. On the fifth
> day, drink a glass of milk or water, and say a boy's name, first
> and last, and within two days, he will ask you out or say, "I like
> you." This is not a joke! It has worked for many, many years,
> and if you break this chain letter, you will have bad luck with
> boys.*

I doubt it! It doesn't matter if the chain letter started in
1677 . . . it has no power at all to make you a more positive,
likable, attractive, productive, or godly person.

What do you depend on to help you achieve success in life?
The Bible has a very definite take on the question:

> This book of the law shall not depart from your mouth, but
> you shall meditate on it day and night, so that you may be
> careful to do according to all that is written in it; for then
> you will make your way prosperous, and then you will
> have success.[5]

What's the secret of achieving a successful and fruitful life? It all comes down to what you do with God's words.

Do you want to make your way prosperous? Would you like to experience success in all that you do? If so, God says you need to put His Word into your heart, meditate on it, and then do what it says by tapping into the power of the Holy Spirit. If you want success, that's how to get it.

Jesus said essentially the same thing. He explained that His Father uses His Word to prune us in order to make us fruitful. Listen to His description of what makes for a successful life:

> I am the true vine, and my Father is the vinedresser. Every branch in Me that does not bear fruit, He takes away; and every branch that bears fruit, He prunes so that it may bear more fruit. You are already clean because of the word which I have spoken to you. Abide in Me, and I in you. As the branch cannot bear fruit of itself unless it abides in the vine, so neither can you unless you abide in Me. I am the vine, you are the branches; he who abides in Me and I in him, he bears much fruit.[6]

Jesus is claiming that as you remain in Him and His words remain in you, there will be an obvious activity of the Father flowing through your life. Your desires become the Father's desires. Your heart becomes the Father's heart. And everyone will be able to see the Father at work through you.

> If you abide in Me, and *My words* abide in you, ask whatever you wish, and it will be done for you. . . . You are already clean because of *the word*.[7]

The Father's main tool for pruning you—and so helping you to enjoy a deeply satisfying, productive life—is the Word of God. The devil knows that if he can keep you from the Word, you'll simply dry up.

Have you experienced that? I have. When we dry up, fruit tends to disappear from our lives.

That's why the devil never attacks your fruitfulness; instead, he attacks your relationship with the Lord by trying to keep you away from the Word. As you dry up, you become more vulnerable to temptation. Suddenly this tawdry thing looks like a good option, or that unhealthy relationship looks enticing, or those skewed ways of thinking seem right.

Everything becomes negotiable. Remember this: *If the devil can keep you away from the Word, he steals the Father's main tool for fruitfulness in your life.* Someone once said to me, "Wayne, the Word will keep you from sin, but sin will keep you from the Word. You choose."

Let God's Word bear fruit in your life. Make your way prosperous and successful by spending time in God's Word, carefully listening for what He wants to say to you.

THE WORD ENABLES YOU TO RECOGNIZE HIS VOICE

Jesus illustrated this when He spoke of a shepherd with his flock. The sheep follow the shepherd "because they know his voice. But they will never follow a stranger; in fact, they will run away from him because they do not recognize a stranger's voice."[8]

And how do sheep know the shepherd's voice?

They know it because they hear it so much.

They've heard him sing as he leads them across the hills and fields. They've heard his comforting tones in the night when coyotes are howling in the distance. They recognize his familiar tone and timbre. They know his common phrasings. They know his voice's usual pace; how it rises in the presence of danger and how it goes silky soft in the presence of hurt. They know its authority, its confidence, its care and concern. And though they will follow that voice anywhere, they will not follow a stranger; they don't know his voice.

Years ago bank tellers were trained to detect counterfeit one-hundred-dollar bills. Trainers put the tellers in a room and showed them the genuine currency. They held classes and seminars to teach the tellers about the almost indistinguishable, almost imperceptible patterns in the real article. The tellers would smell the genuine bills, run their fingers across the fiber and the ink, almost taste them.

Then, when the trainers thought the tellers were ready, they tested them. They put the tellers in front of a conveyor belt loaded with genuine bills. A supervisor, without being seen, would occasionally insert a counterfeit bill onto the belt. The tellers would immediately look at it, pull it off, and say, "I don't know what's wrong with this one, but it's not genuine. Something's not right. Nope, this one looks funny."

How did they recognize the counterfeit bills so quickly? Is it because they studied the fakes? No, it's because *they took a long time to study the real thing.*

In a similar way, we can distinguish between counterfeit voices and the actual voice of the Lord in only one way: We need to know His voice *very well.*

When we know intimately even the smallest, faintest facets of God's genuine character, we'll be able to detect a counterfeit voice at once. The only way to develop that kind of familiarity is through a consistent exposure to God in His Word. Only by sitting with the Divine Mentor will we ever get to know Him intimately and become able to recognize the voice of an imposter.

Paul tells us, "Satan himself masquerades as an angel of light. It is not surprising, then, if his servants masquerade as servants of righteousness."[9] Why else do you think Jesus warned us, "False Christs and false prophets will appear and perform great signs and miracles to deceive even the elect—if that were possible"?[10]

So again, how do we learn to properly identify God's voice? How can we detect a counterfeit, an imposter, a fraud?

The best way I know of is to prepare in advance each time you open God's Word, recognizing that in its pages you are hearing Him. The more you read, the more you are learning to recognize His voice.

THE WORD HELPS YOU MAKE WISE DECISIONS

Did you know that you make approximately three hundred decisions each day?

What time will I get up?

Will I hit the snooze button when the alarm rings?

What will I wear?

What will I have for breakfast?

What will I tackle first at work?

And on it goes. Decision after decision after decision.

Of those three hundred decisions, perhaps 10 percent, or thirty decisions, will have potentially life-altering ramifications. Which relationships should I pursue? What college should I attend? Is it time to start a family? Should I consider that job offer? Do I try to beat this red light?

As you weigh all those options, you're going to draw, from *some* well, the information and the motivation that mobilizes your choices. Into which well will you send down your bucket? If it's not the right well, beware. Maybe it's hormones . . . or a secret fantasy . . . or the insistent voice of the flesh . . . or peer pressure . . . or fear . . . or defensiveness.

By the time you graduate from high school, statistics say you will have watched more than sixteen thousand hours of television. You will have spent fourteen thousand hours in an educational institution. And if you go to church for just two hours a week, you will have spent under two thousand hours getting spiritual help. So, to draw on, when it comes time to make a decision, you'll have eight times as much TV and seven times as much "world and culture and education" as you'll have of church.

Can you see the problem? There's no substitute for drawing from the well of God's Word!

> If you need wisdom, ask our generous God, and he will give it to you. He will not rebuke you for asking. But when you ask him, be sure that your faith is in God alone. Do not waver, for a person with divided loyalty is as unsettled as a wave of the sea that is blown and tossed by the wind.[11]

God gives us His wisdom as we linger in His Word. As it becomes a part of us, increasingly we will know that *this* is the right decision to make or *that* is the right thing to say. We'll know not only what is wrong and what is right, but what is wise and what is foolish.

In our beginning stages as a Christian, we will wrestle with right and wrong. And we should. It will take our hearts and minds some time to debate difficult and challenging issues and questions. But once these have been settled, we graduate. Most of us will not stumble over things *right and wrong* but rather over those that are *wise or unwise*.

Some time ago a great Christian friend called me and said, "Wayne, I'm done! My marriage is finished."

"What's going on?" I asked.

"I didn't *mean* to do anything wrong," he said. "I *wasn't* doing anything wrong."

"That's good," I said.

"But I'm finished. I'm in deep weeds."

"So what happened?"

He proceeded to tell me a story that, with a few changes, could be repeated over and over again, from the stories of many.

"It was innocent, I tell you! You see, a girl in my office was going through a problem at home. She just needed someone to talk to. So we had some lunch at a nearby restaurant, and after our meal we sat in my car in the parking lot. We sat there for a while. I guess a few things I said must have helped her, because she leaned over and gave me sort of a thank-you kiss on the lips. And just then, my wife drove by!"

"You *are* finished!" I said.

"But I didn't do anything *wrong!*" he objected.

"No," I said, "but you sure were *unwise.*"

"Wayne . . . what in the world am I going to do?"

Do you know what my friend's real problem was? Although he wasn't operating in the realm of right or wrong, he failed in the area of wise and unwise.

I said, "Your lack of wisdom started at the office when you gave yourself to this, instead of listening and handing her over to another sister or referring her to a counselor. You took on that job and went from one foolish step to another. No, you didn't do anything wrong. But you did something very unwise."

It took my friend eight months to rebuild his wife's trust. What made it even more difficult for him was that he'd been making unwise decisions all along. By the time this last incident took place, his marriage already teetered on a very fragile foundation.

Remember: Wisdom doesn't have to come at a high price. In fact, many have already paid the exorbitant tuition to enroll in the school of hard knocks. Now they await our audience so they might transfer that wisdom to us.

Wisdom cost Samson his marriage, his family, his ministry, and both of his eyes. The wisdom he garnered from that pain he holds in trust for you and me. We have only to visit with him for those gems to be deposited on our behalf.

David paid dearly for the wisdom he accumulated. It cost him a son, Absalom. It cost him his wives being defiled by Absalom. It cost him his infant son with Bathsheba. Insights that we can't possibly afford—they're ours for receiving. The classroom is set; the instructors wait for their students.

GOD IS SMARTER THAN WE ARE

We don't know what God knows. The sooner we accept this, the better off we'll be. Listening recently to my friend Isaiah, he reminded me again what God said: "For as the heavens are higher than the earth, so are My ways higher than your ways and My thoughts than your thoughts."[12]

On a human level, it's like a first-grader telling Pyotr Ilyich Tchaikovsky he doesn't think his music has amounted to much. A fourteen-year-old basketball player saying Michael Jordan couldn't shoot. A twenty-four-handicap golfer criticizing Tiger Woods' swing.

Yet we still think that God doesn't have much to say . . . and if He does, it's more a take-it-or-leave-it option.

We rashly take matters into our own hands. We maneuver and manipulate to get what we want. We know it's not really the best, yet we'll show people the results and say, "Look what God gave me!"

Again, that's backward:

I will instruct *you* and teach you in the way you should go.
I will counsel *you* and watch over you.[13]

The sooner we accept coaching from biblical mentors God has assigned to us, the better off we'll be. How much better to find a problem with our car by having a professional look it over ahead of time than to be kicking tires on the side of the highway, cursing the automaker.

During a visit to an automotive shop I noticed an interesting sign:

If you bring in your car BEFORE it breaks down, so we can

do the maintenance, the rate is $30.00 an hour. If you wait until it breaks and then you bring it in, the rate is $50.00 an hour. And if it broke, and you tried fixing it yourself, and now you bring it in, it's $120.00 an hour.

Someone once said to me, "The secret of growing in divine wisdom is to come to God stupid. Tell Him you don't know a thing. Tell Him you need to know how to think, how to tie your shoes, how to win friends and influence anybody!"

With that kind of heart, God does His best work. When He is looking for receptacles of divine wisdom, He looks for "PHDs": those who are *Poor, Hungry, and Desperate!*

These are the people who fuel the excitement of our divine mentors. Like the fabled guardians of the Holy Grail, they've been anticipating our company. Let's not keep them waiting.

HOW TO
LISTEN
FOR GOD'S
VOICE

5

One Thing
for Martha

*My dear Martha, you are worried and upset over
all these details! There is only one thing worth
being concerned about. Mary has discovered it,
and it will not be taken away from her.*[1]

There's never enough time in the day for life, is there? A few weeks ago I returned from a ten-day trip to Australia, and when you traverse the globe, "time" can do strange things. I left on a Sunday evening, and I arrived back home on Sunday morning. It was living the old Beatle's tune, "Eight Days a Week." That week, I would have an extra day!

But seven days later, I was no further ahead than when I began. I still needed more time to accomplish what I wanted to.

Time will not wait. It cannot be borrowed. You cannot buy time. It ruthlessly hastens by without afterthought. We can either find the most priority investments or we can squander our resources; time will confiscate every minute we leave idle.

Returning for a moment to the Mary/Martha story, let's just say that Martha was the original Martha Stewart. Completely irritated and frustrated with her sister for not helping out in the kitchen (there Mary was, sitting at Jesus' feet, just listening to Him speak—as if there weren't enough things to be done!), Martha blustered that she shouldn't have to shoulder the load alone. But when she complained, the Teacher lovingly told her that there's one thing better, and that this one thing is what's needed.

Only one thing.

Mary had found the headwaters of life, the source of heaven's artesian well. The unambiguous Source for the Christian—that which fuels, ignites, guides, sustains, and empowers absolutely *everything*—is time with the Master. Quiet, reverent, unhurried moments in the presence of Christ, just as Mary modeled for us. "The words that I have spoken to you are spirit and are life," Jesus declares to us.[2]

One who apparently "got" this lesson was the apostle Paul, for in the little book of Philippians he describes his life's desire: "That I may know Him and the power of His resurrection and the fellowship of His sufferings, being conformed to His death; in order that I may attain to the resurrection from the dead."[3]

What was the Source? Clearly, just as for Mary, it was to "know Christ." And how did Paul plan on drawing near to Jesus? What was his strategy for coming to better know his Savior? Fortunately for us, he outlined it shortly thereafter: "One thing I do: Forgetting what is behind and straining toward what is ahead, I press on toward the goal to win the prize for which God has called me heavenward in Christ Jesus."[4]

Amazing. First Jesus tells us, "Only one thing is needed." Then Paul writes, "One thing I do."

Could anything be that simple?

Jesus didn't say, "Just ten things are needed," nor did Paul say, "Fifteen things I do." When life comes down to its most basic issues—when you "boil life down to the nubbies," as Chuck Swindoll used to say—the Bible makes it very basic for us.

It's just one thing.

Getting back to the Source.

PLAYING SCALES

Watch renowned performers. All top-shelf athletes have a training regimen they repeat day in and day out, again and again and again. Singular regimens will be repeated without apology, and in many ways their practices may be seemingly unconnected with what they will do under the spotlights.

A world-class athlete gets up every morning and does a certain caliber of core exercises. Jerry Rice, one of football's all-time greats, said during his playing days, "I may be able to run and receive passes, but I also do a thousand sit-ups every day."

Concert pianists best illustrate this. No matter the status the artist might have, he will always do one certain activity every day.

One thing . . . scales.

Major scales, minor scales, the Aeolian scale, the Locrian. Why?

Ignace Jan Paderewski was a renowned Polish pianist who lived in the first half of the twentieth century. When his government requested that he play concerts in order to raise money, Paderewski, a patriot and willing citizen, replied: "I will be part of the war effort under one condition. You must allow me every day to continue playing scales, three hours a day. Pay me for eight hours; but I will play scales for three."

They didn't hesitate to accept his offer.

Why would someone of Paderewski's enormous talent insist on playing scales for three hours *daily*? He had a ready answer.

"If I skip one day of scales," he explained, "when I play in concert, I notice it. If I skip two days of scales, my coach will notice. And if I skip three days, the world will notice."

Regularly playing scales develops and maintains the dexterity of a performer's fingers. It gives him the ability to move through the most difficult pieces with speed and accuracy. Whatever the score may call for, with the right practice, he will play it with confidence and skill.

Without a regular diet of scales, the pianist might open up a difficult score (sometimes, even an easy one) and see an ocean of black marks on a sea of white. He braves the punctuated storm only with continued, fumbling struggle—and perhaps not a little embarrassment.

Every disciple who has enrolled in wisdom's life-course does scales. Daily, consistently, with committed fidelity. Mary taught me this discipline. Coupled with Jesus' commendation, her example increases its importance.

DAILY DEVOTIONS

To achieve success, to be productive, to feel satisfied and ful-filled—to become an important part of the solution rather than a significant part of the problem—we must practice the same regimen, day in and day out.

Daily devotions.

When you miss your devotions one day, you notice. When you miss them two days, your spouse and kids notice. And when you miss them three days, the world notices.

When you and I skip our "scales," in no time at all we start falling back on worldly knowledge and wisdom. We may not even realize that's what we're doing, but it's almost inevitable.

Furthermore, we get spiritually weak. If we go without food for several days, how do we start to feel and act? We get cranky, suffer headaches, become abnormally edgy. Starvation causes us to make chaotic choices. Every action is imbalanced; every motive skewed. Neglecting to feed our spirit and ignoring the hunger of our soul causes spiritual weakness; this results in des-perate decisions and stinking thinking!

A starved soul and a famished heart will find you in a party . . . a pity party. The surroundings? A pitiful dump.

Regularly and consistently practicing our scales will embolden us to climb out of the landfill and exchange our odorous clothes for a fragrant wisdom that will mentor us away from the slippery slopes that snared us in the first place.

CORRECTING BACK TO THE SOURCE

I finally relented. I signed up for two weeks of golf lessons. I had built my game entirely on trial and error. I learned simply by watching others, and when I blistered the ball down the fairway, I felt great. But I couldn't tell you *why* it went so far and straight. Then, on the very next tee, more often as not, my ball would discover new territory . . . bounce into the adjacent fairway . . . sometimes even hit a house. And I could never tell you what went wrong. I would just play the probabilities; some days I would feel like Tiger Woods, other days I would be *in* the woods.

I became somewhat fatalistic about golf . . . like the old Doris Day hit from the '50s "Que Sera, Sera."

My coach, however, wasn't buying any of this. He seemed to think it had less to do with fate and more to do with my basic swing. Imagine that!

So for two solid weeks he drilled me in the basics. Nothing else. He wanted me to develop the groove of what a correct swing should feel like. No *whatever will be, will be* with him. He was convinced that learning the foundational mechanics would have a direct impact on my game.

Why did he limit our lessons to the basics? So that when I sliced the ball, I would know *why* I sliced it, and when I hooked it, *why* it happened. And most important, how to correct back without having to repeat the error over and over until some divine miracle occurred to restore my drives to the fairway directly in front of me.

You can hit a good shot without knowing the correct mechanics, but you won't know why you hit it well. You also won't be able to ensure that you hit it that way again anytime soon.

But when you know how to get back to the basics, everything straightens out.

In the Christian life, daily devotions will correct you back to what's right. Not necessarily *who's* right, but *what's* right. For when you do make a mistake: Daily time in God's Word is a divine Global Positioning System to teach you how to find your way back to where you got off the path.

DON'T SKIMP ON THE BASICS

I heard about one young man who wanted to make a living in construction. He had the talent for it but not much money, so he bought some tools at a discount outlet. He got hired on at a job site and seemed to be doing fine. A day or two into the project, however, the foreman inspected his work and discovered that everything he'd done was slightly askew. Despite his hard labor, they had to redo everything he had touched, on the company's time and dollar.

The frustrated foreman called him in and said, "Son, I know you can do good work. But I have to let you go. You're costing us too much money."

What could the young man say? He knew he was to blame; *he just didn't know what he could have done differently*. He picked up his tools and turned to leave.

"Wait a minute," the foreman said. "Let me see your tape measure."

When he laid his own tape measure alongside the young man's, the source of the trouble immediately became clear.

"Where did you get this thing?" the foreman asked.

When the dejected young man told his boss about the discount store, the foreman replied, "Well, that's your problem. You bought a cheap tape measure. It's wrong. Son, in the future, don't skimp on the basics. When those are wrong, everything you do will be wrong."

The young man's tool wasn't off by much. Hardly noticeable at first, maybe, but had he continued to work with that faulty tape measure, the problems would have compounded and magnified. Gradually they would have escalated into a full-blown fiasco.

Life is like that.

When you continue down a path that's skewed—even slightly—you may find catastrophe or chaos gaining on your heels no matter how hard you try to outrun them.

A basic logical theorem says that if your starting premise is incorrect, then every subsequent conclusion will have a high percentage of also being incorrect. For example, if you think one plus one equals three, then every equation involving that premise will lead to a faulty conclusion. When a basic presupposition is wrong, then everything that proceeds from that basic understanding may be equally flawed, no matter how sincere you may be.

In the Christian life, the Bible is your basic premise. You may have a favorite contemporary author or media personality, but he or she can never substitute for the original. I suspect all of us are off by at least an eighth of an inch, and most of us can't claim to be even that close. You have to correct back to the original, to God's Word. This is your primary Source.

No Immunity From Pain . . . Only Wisdom

The mentors of the Bible won't exonerate you from the pains of life. There are necessary hurts that soften the heart, turn us toward compassion, and deepen humility. However, regularly sitting at the Lord's feet will keep you from *unnecessary* suffering. It will prevent you from bringing needless pain upon yourself.

Suppose you have an angry encounter with your spouse. Without knowing what a healthy biblical marriage should be, you have no idea how to dial it back. You flounder with trial-and-error attempts, and by the time you finally get something to work, you're both badly bruised. Wandering aimlessly through the forest when you're off the proven path can leave each of you gasping for air, overly cautious about connection and intimacy, and dubious about each other's sincerity and intentions.

Again, being in the Bible every day installs within us a self-correcting mechanism, a spiritual GPS. Having this in place and finely calibrated, when something does go wrong, we know why it went wrong and, best of all, how to correct back before we are down the path of no return.

We can't afford *not* to sit at His feet as a daily regimen. Because each day will have its own challenges, doing devotions should not be our last thought but our first. This life essential cannot be a burden; we must make it a joy . . . an everyday joy.

Wherever I happen to be in the world, people know exactly what I'm doing—so long as it's 6:30 A.M. my time.

My son, Aaron, who is now a young pastor, has developed the same habit. Every once in a while I'll call him at 6:30 A.M. and say, "Good morning! Where are you doing devotions today?" Likewise, he'll occasionally call me at 6:30 and ask the same thing. It's our custom. It's another special link between us, no matter where we are.

I don't want my son to copy me, necessarily. I just want him to tap into the same Source I tap into each day.

And it isn't original with us, of course. Millions of believers throughout history have had the same custom. They all got their living water from the same well.

He came out and proceeded *as was His custom* to the Mount of Olives.[5]

Jesus *often* withdrew to lonely places and prayed.[6]

Devotions were a habit for Jesus. Every day He spent time with the Father. Everyone around Him knew this was His personal custom. They would say, "Jesus? Oh yes, I know where He is. He's out there somewhere in the hills, having His quiet time. It's His custom. He never misses."

People knew Jesus by the things He was accustomed to doing on a daily basis. He was consistent; everyone knew it. That's what makes Him so trustworthy.

If someone were to describe who you are by your habits, would one of those habits be your daily quiet time? You can celebrate God in a crowd, but you can only get to know God one on one. It's hard to hear His voice in a multitude or when surrounded by distractions. You need alone time with Him, time in solitude where you can really hear His heart.

Each culture has its own customs. As the people of God, let's make this one ours. Jesus started us off. Let's correct back to Him.

WHAT PLEASES GOD

Sometimes I spend time with Enoch, another of my mentors. The Bible says, "Enoch lived 365 years. Enoch walked with God; then he was no more, because God took him away."[7]

In the New Testament we're told: "By faith Enoch was taken from this life, so that he did not experience death; he could not be found, because God had taken him away. For before he was taken, he was commended as one who pleased God."[8]

The Bible doesn't say for sure, but I have an idea that Enoch and the Lord got together at the same time or times every day. I picture them taking long walks together along the pathways of the young earth, Enoch opening his heart to God about everything, God enjoying the kind of relationship He'd had with Adam and Eve back in the garden.

Then there came a day when the Lord said something like *"Enoch, I love this so much! Why don't you just come on home with Me; we'll continue this over on the other side."*

Walking with God was probably a habit Enoch had cultivated since he was a young man (which, of course, may have been around eighty or ninety in those days!).

Speculation aside, the point is, I'm sure Enoch looked forward to those times. They became the highlight of his day.

DEVELOPING THE HABIT

Building a habit like this can be fun. If the new habit isn't something you're used to doing, then link it up with something you enjoy. For example, I enjoy good coffee. So in the morning I link up to a good cup of coffee and a scone at the local café where I have my devotions. All of it, together, has become an enjoyable habit. *Coffee . . . scone . . . my Bible and journal.* It all flows together in my mind. I look forward to my time with my mentors in that shop. It's the highlight of my day . . . and I'm pretty sure the Holy Spirit and my best friends all look forward to it too.

Anna, my wife, links up her time with a steaming cup of tea in the quietness of the evening. She switches on a cozy lamp, sips on her tea, reads the Word, and writes in her journal. I often see her with her Bible, enjoying the day as it closes. Those will be warm memories in my heart for many years to come.

Experts say it takes twenty-one days to develop a habit. I want to encourage you for the next three weeks to cordon off about forty minutes of your morning or evening and take the time to delve into the Word of God, listening for what the divine mentors have been waiting to tell you.

Remember, daily time with the Lord is the Christian's "practicing the scales." The assignments God gives to you and me will become less difficult for us in proportion to our faithfulness in sitting every day before His feet, listening to His Word.

Spiritual maturity comes in layers. Establish a daily time as one of your life priorities. Blend it with something you enjoy, and then begin to do it every day.

ONE OFFENSIVE WEAPON

The sixth chapter of Ephesians describes the spiritual armor God has provided for His children. It speaks of the helmet of salvation, the breastplate of righteousness, the belt of truth, the shield of faith, and shoes that are the preparation (readiness) of the gospel of peace.[9]

Did you happen to notice that all those pieces of armor are for *defensive* purposes? The passage mentions only one weapon for offense: *"The sword of the Spirit . . . the word of God."*[10]

If we're going to be leaders in our families, our communities, and our churches, then we must become a people who know how to take ground and move forward. To do that effectively, you will have to know God's Word and learn how to use it effectively. You will need to know where crucial passages are and memorize key verses.

> It will be pleasant if you keep them [the words of the wise] within you, that they may be ready on your lips.[11]

Use the sword of the Spirit to renew your mind. The point isn't buying a beautiful Bible with gilded edges but being able to effectively use it. If you can't, you'll spend the lion's share of your life on the defensive.

If any athletic team's only goal is "keeping the other team from scoring too much on us," they're history. It's a defeatist's objective to simply lose by fewer points this game than the last one.

If all you're doing is playing defense, if all you're hoping for is to keep from being embarrassed again, then you'll continue to lose. Victory only comes to those who learn how to go on offense and then succeed on the offensive. That's exactly what the Word of God is designed to help you do.

KNOW YOUR OWN WEAPON

Get intimately acquainted with your own Bible, much like you would get accustomed to your own musical instrument. For example, when I play, I want *my* guitar. I have it set up so that I can close my eyes and still know where everything is. If I pick up someone else's guitar, the strings are at a different height, there's a different weight balance, the gauge of strings is odd, the body is bigger and thicker, and the whole thing might exude a different sound.

It's still a guitar, yet it's not *my* guitar.

You need to know your Bible and how to navigate through it.

The Bible calls itself your sword, and if you're about to go into battle, you'd better know your weapon: how it fits your hand, how it feels when you swing it, and what outcome will result for anything it's wielded against. You wouldn't think of going into battle with a plastic sword you bought at a toy shop. Knowing *about* your weapon is no comparison to knowing *how to use it*! In the heat of battle, it doesn't matter if you know who published your Bible or who added the study notes.

What you have hidden in your heart will be the litmus test.

When you archive the Word of God into your heart, securing His words in its inner chambers, the Holy Spirit promises to bring back all He's taught you.[12] For Him to do this, you first have to pack it away; you must store it securely in your archives . . . then it will be ready on your lips.

What do you have stored on the memory card of your heart? If you wonder, try writing down all the references of Scripture that you've memorized on a sheet of paper. How many will that list yield? Is it more than John 3:16?

The Spirit of God promises to bring truth back to your remembrance, but there has to be something archived for Him to bring back!

Jesus was ready when the devil came to tempt Him.[13] Time after time, when Satan made an enticing proposal, Jesus said, *"It is written,"* and then He went on the offensive with particular Scripture passages. Satan had no choice but to flee.

It is the Word of God, the sword of the Spirit—your only offensive weapon in this spiritual conflict—that will be your protection, that will buoy you up and give you the strength and confidence you need for victory. Remember, we don't have the necessary wisdom to win this battle, so we must draw the needed wisdom from somewhere else. That's exactly what the Bible, God's *biblos* ("library"), is for. Store it in your heart, and you will gain wisdom beyond your lifetime.

A Personal Testimony

"Be still," the Lord tells us, "and know that I am God."[14]

If we're going to hear Him effectively, we cannot afford to skimp on our daily devotions. We must, as Mary did, *choose* the one thing that will affect absolutely everything else. It needs to be established and guarded with utmost sincerity; out of that sacred enclosure in our life, God will show up, and He *will* speak.

The inception of New Hope Christian Fellowship in Hawaii came with this in mind. I knew we needed to get out of the blocks correctly. I knew we needed to hear from God every day, every step of the way. Five months before we began, I called our administrator and said, "We must be hearing from God for every step we take. So would you meet with me each morning at 6:30, and we will do devotions together? We'll read through the Bible systematically, and then when God speaks to us about some aspect we need to give attention to, we'll write it in a journal and talk about what He's saying. We'll then define how we will be different today because of what God just said to us."

He readily agreed.

So that's what we did. For the next year and a half we met every morning—and out of that sacred experience, New Hope was born.

Today we do all we can to encourage each attendee to develop the daily habit of devotions. We provide instruction, share success stories, read from our own journals, and distribute copies of our *Life Journal*. All of this makes the whole process simple and readily available.

A BOOK THAT WILL CHANGE YOUR LIFE

Have you ever seen the movie *The NeverEnding Story?* The opening scene takes us to an alley where we meet the main character, a young boy named Bastian. To avoid being bullied, he runs into an old bookstore owned by an old man named Coreander. As Bastian loiters, his attention is captured by a special book.

"What's that book about?" asks Bastian.

"Oh, this is something special," replies Coreander.

"Well, what is it?" says the curious boy.

The old man again evades the question. "Look. Your books are safe. While you're reading them you get to become Tarzan or Robinson Crusoe."

"But that's what I like about them," says Bastian.

"Yes, but afterwards you get to be a little boy again."

"What do you mean?"

"Listen," Coreander instructs, motioning for the boy to come nearer. "Have you ever been Captain Nemo, trapped inside your submarine while the giant squid was attacking you?"

"Yes."

"Weren't you afraid you couldn't escape?"

"But it's only a story," protests the boy.

"That's what I'm talking about. The ones you read are safe."

To which Bastian says, "And that one isn't?"

That's the kind of book God has given to us. I have discovered that the Bible is not a *safe* book. When I read it, I enter it . . . and it challenges me, provokes me, and changes me. I cannot remain the same.

The Bible is not safe. It is eternal.

The Bible is not a passing thought. It is God's final decision.

The Bible is not *a* story. It is *my* story . . . it is *your* story.

Securing Your Devotion

// SCRIPTURE

This I say for your own benefit; not to put a restraint upon you, but to promote what is [appropriate] and to secure undistracted devotion to the Lord. (1 Corinthians 7:35)

// OBSERVATION

An undistracted devotion—that's the highest devotion of all! It's so easy to get distracted. So many things going on that filtering out unnecessary things seems to become more and more difficult . . . especially when the "unnecessaries" are marketed so well. Things that are good but not strategic, nice but not eternal—these can take up the lion's share of my life.

// APPLICATION

The Scriptures tell me that devotion to God is something I must *secure*. Like locking up a bicycle lest it be stolen, or securing a boat to a dock lest it drift, so too I must "secure undistracted devotion to the Lord." I cannot take this for granted. Not securing it invites both theft and drifting. Not securing my devotion to Christ invites the enemy to steal it.

I not only must make my devotions a habit but I also must guard that time. I must not allow appointments or busy days to steal my devotions.

And looking at devotion in the larger sense, I must not let anything cause me to compromise or let down my guard. My devotion to Christ cannot be distracted by what Paul (see 1 Corinthians 7) tells me about—women, emotional affairs, or anything of that nature. I become devoted to my wife, and consistent in my times before God, by filtering and pruning constantly anything not eternally fruitful. In doing so, I secure undistracted devotion.

// PRAYER

Lord, help me to guard my time with You. It's so easy to let an appointment or a ministry activity take its place. Thank You for reminding me often.

6

Five Things for Life

This is what the Lord, the God of Israel, says:
"Write in a book all the words
I have spoken to you."[1]

There are countless bytes of information mesmerizing the airwaves each day. The seemingly infinite array constantly inundates us. It's bouncing off you right now as you read these words. You're completely unaware of this cyber-barrage of signals: radio waves, gamma waves, microwaves, television signals, satellite transmissions. You can neither hear them nor see them unless you can tune in!

These information frequencies pass through us painlessly, completely undetected. Yet thanks to the wonders of modern technology, and with the kind assistance of a radio or TV (among many other devices), we can capture them. They're then translated into understandable images and data. In this way we're able to hear and/or see these frequencies come alive as digitally enhanced sounds and sights.

But there's a far greater frequency that most people never receive. It doesn't contain the latest music trend, nor does it deliver the most popular sitcom. Instead, it's filled with eternal direction and indispensable wisdom.

This frequency holds vital information about your future. It contains the wisdom you'll need in the weeks, months, and years to come. It captures the insight you'll desperately need today. It contains warnings to help you avert pitfalls and crash courses on people skills . . . the very ones you'll need tomorrow at the office!

Isaiah, reminding us of this, speaks out of experience not theory:

> Your ears will hear a word behind you, "This is the way, walk in it," whenever you turn to the right or to the left."[2]

God's mentors stand ready to instruct, coach, remind, and sometimes reprimand. Are we ready to listen? Are we ready to capture what they have for us?

We live in a fast-forward society where we want wisdom that comes in five-second sound bytes. Busyness is often equated with success. We've bought into the myth that hyper-activity is somehow synonymous with "importance."

You have the newest cell phone? You're a step behind—there's already a newer one. And seriously, how could a PDA and a Bluetooth change anyone's value?

Furthermore, with all our devices, do we now listen more effectively? Do they fit the bill? What "media" are the most effective in hearing God's voice above the cacophony of shouts and screams, pitches and pleas?

Let me introduce five.

Are you ready to develop a lifelong habit that will transform the way you think, communicate, and live? Below are the nuts and bolts of how you can effectively develop ears to hear that voice and gain the courage to follow. I carry these five things wherever I go—they've become constant road partners with me over the years. Don't leave home without them.

A carpenter brings his tools. An athlete never forgets his

gear, and a musician never leaves behind his instrument. Avid students of life will attend the University of the Holy Spirit with these five essentials:

(1) Bible
(2) pen
(3) journal
(4) Bible-reading plan
(5) daily planner

When you commit to spending forty minutes a day alone with God, and when you plan to maximize those minutes, you will begin not only to hear but also to capture the wisdom of the ages like never before. It's practical counsel that has been field-tested by believers all over the world.

BRING YOUR BIBLE

I know it sounds novel, maybe even a little shocking, but bring your Bible. Sure, we all love *Our Daily Bread* and *My Utmost for His Highest* and other devotional books. But as wonderful as Christian books, magazines, and devotional aids can be, they're not in the Bible's league. Why not? Because the Bible is the only book God has directly inspired.

All Scripture is inspired by God and is useful to teach us what is true and to make us realize what is wrong in our lives. It corrects us when we are wrong and teaches us to do what is right. God uses it to prepare and equip his people to do every good work.[3]

The Bible is the predominant way God speaks to us. If we put aside that primary channel of divine communication, then soon we will open ourselves to all manner of fanciful thinking. Remember the lady who saw an image of Mary on a grilled cheese sandwich? (It recently sold on eBay for $28,000.) Or did you know that the second coming of Christ has already been spotted in the clouds? The man calling himself the reincarnation of Jesus Christ is a sixty-year-old Puerto Rican from Houston (according to ABC News). His popularity includes hundreds of gullible followers who give money to his cause.

The point is, if we neglect or eliminate God's basic means of speaking to us, we can easily be led off track. Since so many things fly at us at lightning speed, it's crucial we make an appointment each day with our Lord. The Bible is more current than today's newspaper. It's more instructive than the stock report and more helpful than any talk show.

Remember, the Bible is the only book in the universe God has inspired. To "inspire" literally means, "to breathe into."

God's Word is the doorway into His heart and the way to connect with those He's appointed for us. Be sure to bring your Bible to your devotional time. It's the key that opens the gates that need to be open for you this week. God knows what the doors are. He will take care of the opening; you bring the key.

BRING A PEN

Bring a pen with you. Why? So you can mark up your Bible.

You might be thinking, *Why mark up the Bible?* Maybe that even sounds a bit sacrilegious.

Know this: the paper, glue, ink, and leather that together make up the physical book of the Bible are not holy. What God deems holy is what truths I take off the ink and paper and transfer to my heart. *That's* holy.

And this is what the Holy Spirit can bring to life. When I lift God's Word off the page and deposit it into my inmost being, the Lord says, "I will breathe life into it. I will breathe it into your soul. I'll weave it into the very fabric of who you are, and I will change you, from glory to glory, into My image."

The Bible is *not* a magic book.

When I was growing up, we had a gigantic, gilded family Bible that sat on the coffee table. Nobody ever cracked open its pages. We just presented it for all to see, as if its mere presence would ward off the devil as soon as he glimpsed its industrial size.

I had a friend who told me that, as a boy, he used to sleep with the Bible tucked under his pillow to protect him from bad dreams. Nice thought, but God makes no such promises. For the Bible to do you any good, you must pick it up, read it, and absorb its truths into your heart.

When we read the Bible, the Spirit often causes a particular verse or passage to jump out at us. When that happens to me, I take out my pen and I highlight it . . . or circle it . . . or star it . . . or asterisk it . . . or underline it. Sometimes I'll write a date beside it.

What am I doing? I'm simply agreeing with the Spirit: "On this day, the Holy Spirit revealed this to me."

Here's my passion: Every day of my life, I want to do everything I can to draw God's thoughts from the Scriptures' ink and paper and imprint them on my soul. That's when He speaks His words directly into my understanding and breathes His life into my heart.

While the Word sits on the coffee table it's inert; it's just another book. But when we bring it to our eyes and drink it in, the Spirit breathes into it and inspires it into our lives. At that moment, as Paul says, "the eyes of your heart" will be enlightened.[4] The Bible comes to life when I apply its truth to my circumstances and situations.

So get a pen and underline the passages where God seems to be getting your attention. All you're doing is agreeing with what the Spirit is already doing in your heart. One man once told me, "We are poorer because of the opportunities we have missed."

The Holy Spirit is already highlighting passages for you.

With your pen, you can let Him know that you've captured the truth and that you refuse to miss another opportunity to become a little more like Him!

BRING A JOURNAL

A journal is simply a notebook where you can write down what God says to you. That's all that journaling means— writing it down! Let me repeat our opening Scripture for this chapter:

This is what the Lord, the God of Israel, says: "Write in a book all the words I have spoken to you."[5]

Take notes on what God is saying. Treat every word like pure gold. This will help you more than I can begin to describe. Just remember that your journal is not a diary. It is God speaking to you as you daily set aside forty minutes for devotions. It is not a place for random thoughts (although this can be a therapeutic exercise at another level). Your journal is the garnering of wisdom, the gathering place of divine insight you'll receive from the mentors of the ages.

What does journaling look like in practice? The following is a reproduction of my entry after reading Deuteronomy 28:47–48.

Having a Heart to Serve

// SCRIPTURE

Because you did not serve the Lord your God with joy and a glad heart, for the abundance of all things; therefore you shall serve your enemies whom the Lord shall send against you, in hunger, in thirst . . .

(Deuteronomy 28:47–48)

// OBSERVATION

God doesn't want us just to serve Him, does He? No, it's the motives behind my serving that catch His attention.

I can serve out of *fear of retaliation*. I can serve for a *desire to be applauded*. I can serve *to be noticed, rewarded, given credit*, or even *granted recogniton*—but here God says, "I don't want you to serve Me out of mere duty. I want you to serve Me with a joyful and a glad heart." It is the motive and the heart behind what I do that makes what I do life-giving.

It is not for the want of anything. It is simply for the joy of serving. The takeaway is that the joy I have now in my heart for having served is the greatest treasure of all. When I don't have that correct motive, it's like serving my enemies in hunger and thirst.

// APPLICATION

If my motives are wrong in serving, I can still serve; but when I am done, it will leave me hungry and spiritually thirsty. Serving is designed to fill my heart, but if my motives are wrong, I will go away empty, tired, depleted, burned out, and angry that others didn't help me more. . . . I have to change—not my serving, but the heart with which I serve.

// PRAYER

Father, my prayer is this: Please seal this truth to my heart, so that I might be a true servant. Help me to serve with a joyful heart, for indeed the joy of the Lord will be my strength.

Ninety-five percent of all the messages I preach come out of my journals. Just by sitting at His feet and listening to His instruction, I gain the wisdom of the Divine Mentor. After I let it grip my own heart, I place it on a silver platter and serve it to my people.

JOURNALS FOR THE HEART

Many kinds of journals are available. We've developed several at New Hope that work very well. People often prefer the classic we call the *Life Journal*. We also have one called the *First Steps Journal*, which features a little less reading than the classic version. It omits a lot of parallel passages and streamlines the readings but uses the same basic pathway.

In addition there's the *Children's Journal*. For this one we feature what we consider the most important verses from the classic edition. So while the kids are reading three verses from a particular passage, you'll be reading the entire three chapters from which those verses are taken. I also really like the *Children's Journal* because it has cartoon characters throughout, featuring a little dog name Soapy (taken from the acronym *SOAP*, which I'll introduce in chapter 7).

Here's a side benefit to having your children read and journal at the same time you are. If your little daughter is reading a portion of a Bible story—let's say, the account of Noah—she's likely to come to you and say, "Hey Mom, I read about Noah and the ark today!" And you'll be able to say, "I did too!"

Of course, you'll have read a lot more than she did, but she'll still be able to share with you what she's written in her journal. The two of you will be able to tell each other what you've learned about the passage. In that way, you can have real fellowship and share with each other what God is teaching you.

One of the best things I ever did with my son, Aaron, was take him to breakfast and do devotions together. We would read the same passage. Aaron would pick out something that

God had highlighted for him and write it down. I would do the same, and then we would share with one another how God was working in each of us. It's a great way to develop relationships and pray for each other.

The same sort of thing can happen when you and your spouse both journal. Earlier I told you that my wife is an evening person. She does her devotions in the evening, while I do them in the morning. But several times a week she'll call me up and say, "Honey, what did you get out of your reading yesterday?" I'll read my journal entry to her, and she'll read hers to me.

Doing devotions in this way allows you to share with each other what God is speaking into your own lives, and that experience will strengthen your marriage. It encourages you both to sit regularly at the feet of Jesus.

IS JOURNALING REALLY NECESSARY?

Despite all these benefits, I run into many believers who resist the concept of journaling. Some say to me, "Wayne, I read the Bible, but I don't take notes." In response, I often tell them a story.

Several years ago, my friend Jack Hayford and I were both speaking at a conference. At that time Jack pastored a church in Van Nuys, California. I'd been struggling with some issues in the ministry and knew he'd probably gone through something similar. I called his room and asked if we could meet.

"Absolutely!" he said. "But I have to catch a plane in one hour. Can we meet now?"

"Sure," I answered.

"Let's meet in the lobby," he replied.

I grabbed a notebook and headed for the elevator. He was already waiting for me when I arrived.

Right away he graciously reminded me that he had only one hour to give me. For the first five minutes, I described my struggle, giving him enough context to understand my problem. Then I said, "If you could rewind the tape, knowing what you know now, what would you say to me, in terms of advice and counsel?"

For the next fifty-five minutes, he spoke while I listened.

Now, let's switch things around. What if *I* had spoken for most of the hour, then said to Jack, "Okay, you have five minutes. *Go!*" What kind of relationship would that reflect? Would that honor him? On the contrary, what was honoring was that I limited my speech and gave him freedom to speak into my life.

This is how we best honor God in our devotions.

HONORING GOD WITH OUR NOTE-TAKING

He who has an ear, let him hear what the Spirit says to the churches.[6]

I also did something else that day I spoke to Jack Hayford: I took pages of notes. I was serious about getting Jack's help, and I knew his words would not be idle. I knew God would speak through him, and I didn't want to waste the moment.

Do you think my note-taking dishonored him? Hardly! *Taking notes is one of the best ways to pay your instructor a compliment.* To Jack, I was communicating that I intended to do something with his counsel. I was determined and serious about applying what he was instructing.

When I write down God's thoughts in a journal during my devotions, I am saying to Him, "I intend to apply what You are saying to me today." We honor the Holy Spirit and the mentors He's chosen when we take notes on what He says through them.

Some people still object, and some have said to me, "I understand all that, but I still don't take notes. Journaling just doesn't help me that much."

In reply, I usually remind the person that tests are coming. If he or she asks what I mean, I might give an example like this:

"Imagine that we took a physics class together. Imagine I take copious notes, while you don't take any. Now, you might say to me, 'Why are you taking notes? I don't need notes—I just listen to the professor. I already attend the class; why also write down what the professor says?'"

Because, when the tests come—and mark my words, *they will*—which of us do you think will do better?

There isn't any question the tests will come. But as we listen for God's voice in His Word and write down what we hear Him saying to us, His wisdom starts to pour into our hearts, layer by layer. Then, when the hard times collide with our peaceful little world, we will remember far more of what our tutors have told us. We'll connect the dots and navigate our way to victory.

Do you remember how in the book of Deuteronomy God required that Israel's future kings write out the law in their own handwriting and daily read it? Listen to this instruction:

> When he sits on the throne as king, he must copy for himself this body instruction on a scroll. . . . He must always keep that copy with him and read it daily as long as he lives. That way he will learn to fear the Lord his God by obeying all the terms of these instructions and decrees. This regular reading will prevent him from becoming proud.[7]

The way I see it, if God required this of kings, why wouldn't it be a first-rate idea for the King's kids?

BRING A BIBLE-READING PLAN

When you do your devotions, make sure you have a map, or reading plan, that guides you. If you don't move through the Bible with some kind of GPS, you'll find it can be hard to navigate.

Without such a system, where will you start? Most of us look at this big, thick book called the Bible (really sixty-six books) and think, *Where do I begin? Start with page one and read straight through?*

A reading plan gives you a clear path to follow. Without it, you're likely to visit only your favorite places. Novices usually start with the Psalms and Proverbs, then meander through Matthew, Mark, Luke, and John. Then revisit Proverbs once more, and after that maybe a little more from the Gospels. We end up with unturned pages between—pages holding innumerable undiscovered truths and untold buried treasure. On the "Stay With My Favorites" plan, you'll likely wind up with a partial view of who God is and a stack of strange, half-processed viewpoints on any number of issues.

Don't leave Scripture's lesser-visited mentors feeling alone and abandoned!

The loneliest people in the Bible are the Minor Prophets. I can almost hear one complaining: "These Christians *never* come to my house! They visit David and Solomon consistently. They visit the disciples and Paul regularly. Maybe once a year they even visit our eccentric cousin, Jeremiah. But they don't ever come to *my* house." And immediately all the other Minor Prophets shout their agreement: "Amen! Alas, we make much food—yea, even a banquet—and yet they come not!"

Use a map that takes you down all the Bible's side alleys. Go to the prophets' homes and find that they'll greet you with gusto and have a spread you can't believe. The Minor Prophets have major messages for you! But remember, you'll probably never visit them without a neighborhood map.

The *Life Journal Bible Bookmark* takes readers through the Old Testament once and the New Testament twice annually. It's set up in such a way that students can track their daily progress. For some who are just beginning, this can emerge as a seemingly gargantuan starting point. "Is there a reprieve? What if I'm not used to reading three or four chapters a day?"

No problem. Start by reading just half of it. It will very likely be twice as much as you read last year. Then as you get more practice, keep increasing the amount you read.

Miss a day? Don't disqualify yourself, and don't drop out.

Each day, begin with the reading scheduled for that specific day. In other words, if you're behind, stay with the reading designated for that date. When you have a day off or extra time, you can return to what you've missed and catch up. When you don't have time, don't try to rush; don't try to cram three days' worth of reading into one. You'll get nothing out of your day's devotions.

Wherever you are . . . just start! Plunge in. You may feel a bit guilty when you see the blank stares of unfilled accountability boxes. Don't let that guilt settle on you: Leave those spaces to fend for themselves and go to the reading scheduled for that day. Read it slowly. Read it for comprehension.

"What if I get behind by three or four days?"

God will still be waiting to meet you, waiting to reveal His insights and direction, waiting to wrap you in His love.

Don't give up!

We can all remember times when we've been so engrossed in a project that we skipped breakfast and then worked right through lunch. By three or four in the afternoon your hunger begins to scratch at the insides of your stomach. Just then, you remember you've forgotten *two* meals! What do you do—what's your response?

You wouldn't say, "Well, I skipped breakfast, and I breezed right over lunch, so forget it—I'm not eating anymore. After all, I've already forgotten two meals—what's the point?" Of course not! You'd look forward all the more to dinner.

It's the same way here. Remember, you're feeding yourself spiritually. So if you've missed a couple of meals, just eat for that day. Feed yourself, and then keep going. And when you have opportunity, try to pick up what you missed.

It's a good feeling to see your reading plan all filled out when you finish. It's also fun to reward yourself for a job well done. Treat yourself to something and celebrate! (I once even bought myself a motorcycle.)

BRING A DAILY PLANNER

It may seem odd to think of bringing a daily planner to your devotions, but there's a very solid reason for it. What inevitably happens when you start your time with God? *Some unfinished task pops into your mind.* It's utterly predictable.

An unpaid bill. An unsent letter. An incomplete assignment. An errand left undone.

You attempt to log each one in your mind. In an effort to remember, you maybe try mental tricks, using acrostics or repetition so as not to forget them. By the time you're done, you've missed most of what God has spoken to you. Your brain cells were recruited and depleted in the battle to administrate.

A daily planner can be a store-bought calendar . . . or it can take the form of a three-by-five card, a napkin, or the back of an envelope. Then, whenever something random pops into your mind—*return call, send e-mail, run errand for wife*—make a note of it. Then, instantly, you can lay that issue aside and go back to your reading.

When you don't have to use your brainpower to remember trivial things, random thoughts don't have to stay in your mind. You're free to concentrate your best energies on what God wants to say to you through His Word.

And guess what? When you're done, you'll have a precious gem for the ages from Him, *and* all those random things will still be waiting patiently for your attention.

Your heart will be better for it, your mind will be better for it, *and* your wife will let you come home because you did the errand as you promised. It all works out!

STRENGTH FOR THE CHALLENGES AHEAD

If it hasn't come already, the day will come when your world will tighten around you like a vise. Mistakes will threaten to steal your confidence. Serious illness may throw dark curtains across your windows of hope. Grief might grab you by the throat. You will wonder which way to turn, which way to run.

But because you have stood with David at Ziklag, with Moses in the Sinai, with Paul in Athens, and with Esther in Persia, you will know what to do. "Your ears will hear a word behind you, 'This is the way, walk in it,' whenever you turn to the right or to the left."[8]

That will be the voice of Isaiah, a divine mentor you've met along the way.

When you commit to doing daily devotions, come prepared. You don't pack winter coats for a trip to Hawaii, nor do you show up at a dinner party in your pajamas. Five simple things to bring when you meet with your divine mentors:

- •• Bible
- •• pen
- •• journal
- •• Bible-reading plan
- •• daily planner

These will help bring the wisdom of the ages home to your heart.

You can't afford *not* to embark on this journey into eras past, guided by handpicked mentors who await your company. The Lord's counsel will open up whole worlds of understanding. His warnings will save you wasted years, and His encouragement will be like a shaft of golden sunlight, breaking through a curtain of clouds on a gloomy day.

RICHES BEYOND OUR IMAGINATION

How can any of us assign a value to spending quiet, personal time in such a presence? No one could ever over-calculate the treasure of God's daily counsel spoken through the likes of Luke, Joshua, and Samson.

Want to compare it to gold? It's worth more than every ounce in the world. And every day of our lives He waits for us with a fresh supply.

My fruit is better than gold, even pure gold, and my yield better than choicest silver.[9]

Some Assembly Required

// SCRIPTURE

I also will no longer drive out before them any of the nations which Joshua left when he died, in order to test Israel by them, whether they will keep the way of the Lord to walk in it as their fathers did, or not.

(Judges 2:21–22)

// OBSERVATION

Not everything will be done for us. How wonderful, yes, to have been given committed tutors, parents that love us, or the privilege to be under great coaches! But the truth remains that much of life will still be handed to us in its unfinished state: "Some assembly required."

The government provides schooling, but only you can convert that into wisdom and character. You can find a spouse, but only you can assemble a healthy marriage. You may have a child, but quality parenting will require some assembly. You can be hired for a job, but success and advancement is a do-it-yourself proposition.

Israel wanted it handed to them without any requirements.

// APPLICATION

We're often like that, aren't we? We don't really want to pray—we just want the benefits of someone who did. We don't want to make the sacrifices necessary for a healthy marriage—we just want the results.

God leaves "some assembly required" because without it our hearts remain immature, susceptible to guile, and prone to stray. So He lets us face a few battles to stutter our struts. A few setbacks that lower our noses and reintroduce our knees to the floor. These are the marks of a man or woman that God will use: *those whose eyes are wet, whose knees are bent, and whose hearts are broken . . . but now are mended by His grace.*

// PRAYER

Father, I choose to be one of these people. Thank You for the battles You've left behind for me to win . . . for in doing so, my heart is conquered, humbled, and made ready for Your entry.

7

SOAP

*We sometimes tend to think we know all we
need to know to answer these kinds of questions—
but sometimes our humble hearts can help us
more than our proud minds.*[1]

For a lifetime of growth, continual learning is an essential. Experience alone will not guarantee learning. It's what you *learn from* your experiences that will transform your future. Your future is not comprised of the sum total of all your experiences—it will consist of how you have *defined* them.

So what life-learning dictionary do you use? What meaning do you give to each event?

Remember that suffering will change you, but not necessarily for the better. You must choose to grow better not bitter.

Consistently make your learning greater than your experience by defining each occurrence and setback *biblically*. It will save you years of cleanup and miles of burned bridges.

The Bible is God's choice for a life-dictionary. Joseph will help you convert family betrayal into a future of promise. King David will help you through a child's rebellion. Moses will help leaders with complaining staff. Abigail will encourage those with foolish husbands.

ONE PREREQUISITE TO LEARNING

At New Hope we've done any number of things over the years to help our church grow, but one thing we've done stands head and shoulders above everything else.

It has nothing to do with demographics.

It doesn't depend on location.

It isn't triggered by worship style.

It's developing a *self-feeding program,* using a simple system of daily devotions.

Some time ago I read in a medical magazine these poignant words: *The health of twenty-first-century America will no longer be determined by what people get the doctors to do for them, but rather by what doctors can get people to do for themselves.*

Self-feeding will be the heart of a healthy Christian, the heart of a healthy twenty-first-century church. It will be each of us, on a daily basis, recording biblical instructions that contain centuries of wisdom and applying them like an unguent to relational grievances and to life's cuts and bruises.

At the heart of journaling is an easy-to-remember acrostic: *SOAP.*

S = Scripture

O = Observation

A = Application

P = Prayer

Let me describe how SOAP works. It's a basic system that can have profound results. It will help you be productive right out of the chute.

To set the stage, allow me to quote the beautiful words of Psalm 19:9 in the King James Version. It helps us to remember what SOAP is all about: "The fear of the Lord is clean."

S = SCRIPTURE

In the last chapter you read how a Bible bookmark (or some other reading plan) will give you an extended reading from both Testaments for every day of the year. As you peruse the entire scheduled reading for a given day, ask the Lord to bring home to your heart one text in particular.

That is a prayer the Holy Spirit loves to answer.

He will highlight one verse or thought that momentarily stops you in your tracks or seems to shine out from the page. He will whisper, *"This is for you—this is a promise you can hold to"* or *"This instruction will get you back on track."* Whatever the text is, *write it down in your journal.* Copy out the verse at the top of your entry for that day.

Why is it so important to focus on one short text or verse rather than several? Why do I strongly encourage you to find *one thing* the Spirit is saying to you? It's quite simple, and I've seen this borne out time and again: If you try to catch more than that, I guarantee that at the end of the year you'll remember *none* of them. But if you focus on just one a day, by the time December 31 rolls around, you'll have more than three hundred sixty gems packed away in your heart. And that's priceless!

By interacting in this way with the Lord through His Word, you'll be hearing His prophetic voice. *You will begin making permanent decisions based on eternal wisdom, not on temporary setbacks.*

Let God's Word hold you up! Develop a daily discipline of devotions that is unshakable.

During the time I almost dropped out of ministry, I ended up spending some time at a "no talking" monastery in California to regain my physical and spiritual equilibrium. Even though my psyche was fried and my energy depleted, I continued my devotions. If it weren't for the disciplines I'd developed over the years, I doubt I would have found my way home.

It was there, on the verge of cashing it all in, that the Lord spoke once more through Jeremiah: "But as for me, I have not hurried away from being a shepherd after You."[2]

That was His prophetic word for me.

In the midst of that dark, dry time, that single verse spoke more to my heart than volumes of eloquent verbiage. And that verse will always illustrate for me the truth of this one: "A word aptly spoken is like apples of gold in settings of silver."[3]

Allow God to speak that apt word to you by focusing on *one* main thought from your daily reading—not five, ten, or a baker's dozen.

One thing.

O = OBSERVATION

The question is never "Does God speak?" but rather "Am I listening?" To best hear what God has to say to you, you must still your heart.

Set aside your pressing demands.

Turn off all your electronic distractions.

Rarely does God shout to make himself heard!

As the Spirit highlights that one single thought, observe carefully what the verse says. Think about to whom the passage was originally addressed and why it was written. Ponder its meaning, its tone, its purpose. Take several moments to meditate on it, to let its message soak clear through to your heart.

The first and most important commandment of all, according to Jesus, is to "Love the Lord your God with all your heart, and with all your soul, and with *all your mind*."[4] That means He doesn't want you to disengage your brain as you listen for His voice.

Have you ever noticed how often in Scripture God requires His servants to "observe" something in order to learn a divine lesson from it? Ponder just a few examples:

•• "Consider the blameless, observe the upright; there is a future for the man of peace."[5]

•• "Consider how the lilies grow. They do not labor or spin. Yet

I tell you, not even Solomon in all his splendor was dressed
like one of these."[6]

•• "Consider Abraham: 'He believed God, and it was credited to
him as righteousness.' Understand, then, that those who
believe are children of Abraham."[7]

•• "*He* [Jesus] sat down opposite the treasury, and *began observing
how the people were putting money into the treasury; and
many rich people were putting in large sums. A poor widow
came and put in two small copper coins.*"[8]

Now it's your chance to do some careful observing and considering of your own. Ponder the message God has highlighted
for you. Write out in manuscript form what you observe. It may
be only a paragraph or perhaps a few sentences. The important
thing is to put pen to paper and make an observation in your
journal. Take into context the setting and the situation. Make
an observation of what's happening, who's affected, what's taking place. This will increase your comprehension and develop
your observation skills.

A = APPLICATION

After you've carefully observed what the text says, take
some time to write out how you plan to put into practice the
lesson the Divine Mentor has just brought to your attention.
How will you be different today as a result of what you've just read?
Application answers the question, "How does this verse or
thought apply to me?"

Application is a crucial part of this process, for without it,
all you're doing is amassing facts, trivia, and bits of knowledge.
Do you remember what the Lord Jesus thought of that kind of
practice? In a classic confrontation with the Pharisees, He said:
"I know that you are Abraham's descendants; yet you seek to
kill Me, because My word has no place in you."[9]

Have you ever pondered the amazing irony of the Pharisees' relationship with Jesus? They were *bona fide* Jews with prodigious pedigrees. Yet they plotted how to violate the sixth commandment, and then schemed a cover-up by making sure the Romans committed the murder and took His body down from the cross before the Sabbath arrived so the Jews wouldn't defile the day.

Astonishing. The Pharisees had extensive knowledge of and intimate familiarity with the details of God's Word . . . while missing the whole point!

Amassing biblical knowledge without a commitment to applying it to life leads only to massive miscomprehension. Paul agrees: "We know that we all possess knowledge. Knowledge puffs up, but love builds up. The man who thinks he knows something does not yet know as he ought to know."[10]

James created an unforgettable metaphor to say much the same thing:

> Anyone who listens to the word but does not do what it says is like a man who looks at his face in a mirror and, after looking at himself, goes away and immediately forgets what he looks like. But the man who looks intently into the perfect law that gives freedom, and continues to do this, not forgetting what he has heard, but doing it—he will be blessed in what he does.[11]

Application is what seals God's Word to our hearts. Application makes the difference between *hearing* His will and *doing* His will. Application is what sets apart a disciple from a dabbler, a follower from a fan. Application states how you will live differently because of what you've just read.

A powerful force comes into play when we bring "what we believe" and "how we live" closer together. One of Christendom's greatest maladies is the phenomenon of living inconsistently with what we believe. *Incongruence is one of the foremost causes of anxiety.* We espouse one thing yet live another.

- •• We know all there is to know about love, but we aren't known for being loving.
- •• We know all there is to know about joy, but there is no joy in our homes.
- •• We know all there is to know about forgiveness, but we still can't forgive.

Some years ago a pastor friend of mine was carrying on an illicit sexual affair. When it finally came to light, he was reprimanded, summarily dismissed, and put under discipline and counseling. As a friend, I called him one day and asked, "How could you do that?"

"Wayne," he replied, "I don't need more people to condemn me."

I reassured him of my friendship and my heart, but I told him I needed to know how he could tolerate the pain sustained by the massive inconsistency of his lifestyle with his message.

I'll never forget his answer. "Wayne," he said, with a heavy sigh. "I wasn't reading the Bible for life. I studied the Bible only to get sermons out of it. I would find one and immediately give it as a message on Sunday. As soon as I could extract enough lesson material to hand out, I was done for the day. It was never routed through my heart, so it left me starving even though I was overseeing an orchard."

Knowledge alone is no guarantee of growth. But with God's help we can dial in the two lenses of knowledge and application. Clarity appears, and focus results. One of the greatest blessings is promised to those who consistently apply what they know: "If you know these things, *you are blessed if you do them.*"[12]

P = PRAYER

The final stage of your journal entry is recording your prayer. It could read as simply as: *Lord Jesus, help me to be a person who listens to Your Word. Today I will take time to hear what You are saying to me. Speak, Lord, for Your servant is listening.*

Finish your time in the Word with a thoughtful prayer to God. Ask Him to help you apply what you've just learned. And don't forget to tell Him how thankful you are for the power of His Word!

Some people object to writing out their prayers, but I've found this to be a wonderful way to cement everything that's just happened in my mind and heart. Avoid writing your entry in notation form. No CliffsNotes! Write out everything God said to you; when it comes time to pass along what you learned, *everything* will come back—even the prayer you offered to Him.

Sometimes when I return to an old journal entry, I read the prayer portion—and soon I feel convicted by my own prayer. How often I've asked God to return to me the heart I had when I first heard Him. Over the years, our heart can change; it can harden and become calloused. Rereading our own prayers reminds us to keep a supple heart, one that's always pliable in the hands of the Maker.

Once you've written out your prayer, I suggest you return to the top of your entry and give it some descriptive title. Maybe you've highlighted Matthew 10:27, which says: "What I tell you in the darkness, speak in the light; and what you hear whispered in your ear, proclaim upon the housetops."

Give your entry a title like "Listening" or "Ears That Hear." Write it at the top of your entry for that day. Now you have captured a gem in the making. Applying it into the daily-ness of life will make for a vibrant and verifiable faith.

TABLE OF CONTENTS

Finally, it's important to provide a quick notation in the front of your journal about what God spoke to you, and when. The *Life Journal* has a ready-made place for that, in the very front under "Table of Contents."

In your table of contents, write out the title you gave to your entry, along with the Scripture reference, the date, and the journal page where your entry is found.

If three months later you were to ask me what God has been saying to me, I can go to the *Life Journal's* table of contents and find it in seconds. Everything God spoke to me will return. There I have a treasured record of His wisdom, personalized directly to my heart, and it can never be taken away from me.

When God highlights a verse or thought from your daily reading, put some SOAP on it—Scripture, Observation, Application, and Prayer! Then record it in your table of contents. You will hereby give God's truth roots into your soul, and you'll be building a spiritual resource that will enrich your life for years to come.

WHEN YOU'RE AT YOUR BEST

Over the years many people have inquired as to the best time for daily devotions.

I have a very basic answer.

The best time for devotions is when you're at your best.

I'm a morning person, so I do my devotions early, about six-thirty. That's when I'm at my best.

On the other hand, Anna comes alive in the evening. So she usually does her devotions after the sun has gone down, because she wants to give the Holy Spirit the prime moments of her day. In this way she grows more, retains more, and comprehends more.

While her brain is going full speed at 7:00 P.M., mine is shutting down—I'm losing functionality by the second. By the time 10:00 P.M. rolls around, I'm comatose.

My wife and I have different time schedules and different body rhythms. There is nothing wrong with that. I don't buy the one-size-fits-all idea, the concept that if you want *really* good devotions, you have to do them early in the morning.

Do your devotions at *whatever* time is your best time. When you give God your best, that's when class is in session . . . for you.

CREATE SOME FERTILE SOIL

By using this simple SOAP method to journal every day, you'll create fertile soil in your heart. God will plant a seed there, and soon a tree will take root and fruit will come forth:

> How blessed is the man who does not walk in the counsel
>> of the wicked,
> Nor stand in the path of sinners,
> Nor sit in the seat of scoffers!
> But his delight is in the law of the Lord,
> And in His law he meditates day and night.
> He will be like a tree firmly planted by streams of water,
> Which yields its fruit in its season
> And its leaf does not wither;
> And in whatever he does, he prospers.[13]

Bleating Sheep

// SCRIPTURE

When Samuel reached him, Saul said, "The Lord bless you! I have carried out the Lord's instructions." But Samuel said, "What then is this bleating of sheep in my ears?" (1 Samuel 15:13–14 NIV).

// OBSERVATION

God had given Saul instructions to completely eradicate the Amalekites. Instead, Saul decided for himself what should or shouldn't be eliminated. Whether it was greed, or simply an emotional unwillingness, or whatever the reason, he felt his personal evaluations were superior to God's. When Samuel arrived, Saul was straining himself to pat his own back while right behind him were the sounds that showed his disobedience.

// APPLICATION

God will point out what is precious and what is not. Like Saul, I may have the tendency to "improve" on divine decrees, but I must not. *I need to let God establish my priorities.* That will tell me what skills I must develop, and even which risks to take.

In the end God will not hold me accountable for what I have done so much as for how much I have done of what *He has asked me to do.*

I only have limited time and energy to accommodate eternal priorities, so I will garner His instructions, record them, cull unnecessary activities, and follow Him fully. Then I will have the confidence to say, "I have carried out the Lord's instructions" and not hear the bleating of sheep in the background.

// PRAYER

Dear Father: Please help me in this life essential so that I prune correctly to Your priorities. Give me the strength to say no to opportunities that may hold great promise but may also lead me further from Your plans. Help me to carry out Your commands without the bleating of sheep in the background.

When God plants a seed into the fertile soil of an obedient heart, it will certainly grow into something fruitful. On the other hand, a heart that strays from God's Word becomes hardened, and when He drops a seed there, it will take weeks . . . months . . . maybe even years to germinate. Hard ground is counterproductive. Even the very rains that are designed to satisfy the soil's thirst can instead wash away the seed from parched ground, its flow moving the seed of potential toward more porous soil.

Remember what happened to the fearful, lazy servant in the parable of the talents? The master said, "Take away the talent from him, and give it to the one who has the ten talents."[14] Having hard soil can result in what little you have being taken away and given to good soil so it can bear an abundant harvest.

Keep your heart in prime condition by interacting with the Spirit of God and with whomever He chooses to be a divine mentor for you today.

There will be times when you don't understand most of what you've just read. Take heart. You won't be alone in this dilemma. Here's an easy solution: *Don't journal on the 90 percent you don't understand; journal on the 10 percent you do.* If we're not faithful with the 10 percent we understand, why should He reveal to us the 90 percent we do not yet understand?

When we are faithful with what we do know, He will be delighted to reveal to us what we do not yet know.

Let the adventure of a lifetime begin.

8

Fresh Bread

Then Jesus declared, "I am the bread of life.
He who comes to me will never go hungry."[1]

Molokai is not the island most visitors choose when they're contemplating a Hawaiian vacation.

Perhaps they should. Especially if they, like me, love fresh bread.

I get to visit Molokai every so often. Whenever I do, I make it a point to stop by the Kanemitsu Bakery. I don't mean I drop in at my convenience for a pastry. I, along with a dozen others, will stand in an adjacent alley at midnight. Within an hour, a long line queues up behind a weathered door, catching the most alluring aromas wafting out into the starry night.

Fresh bread. Ah! There's nothing like it in the world. Just the smell of it can embolden you to brave this dark Molokai alley in the middle of the night.

At a given time, an employee will open the door, spilling light and more fragrant aroma into the alleyway. He surveys the nocturnal parade and asks the first few in line, "What kind of bread would you like to order?"

Some will pull a list from their pocket and dutifully repeat

Mom's order. Others will buy just enough to satisfy their evening hunger: jelly-filled, rye, sourdough, or some exclusive Hawaiian variety.

"Got it," the attendant will say as he closes the door.

———

A few moments later the door opens again. I have ordered one whole-wheat loaf and one rainbow—a loaf with several pastel colors throughout the dough. The soft, warm bread exchanges hands. I gladly pay the anonymous broker, who then disappears quickly behind the weathered door.

Every night thirty or more people will line up in the alley, each awaiting their share of fresh bread: a special breakfast, gifts for family they will visit on a neighboring island, or simply a midnight delicacy.

———

All over the globe, hungry people are being drawn to fresh bread . . . but a slightly different kind of bread. This one feeds hungry hearts. This bread is the life of the world.

Fresh bread—the Bread of Life—fills our gaping holes. It answers the questions of our soul and satisfies the emptiness of our heart.

This bread is first for the eating, and then for the sharing. One of my favorite mentors confirms this: "Your words were found and I ate them, and Your words became for me a joy and the delight of my heart."[2]

NOTHING WORSE THAN "STALE"

God is very partial to fresh bread. He doesn't care for stale bread because He knows it can't give us the nourishment we require. It might give us opinions and arguments, but those will neither stir our souls nor transform our actions.

The Lord bids us to come daily to *Manna's Bakery* for fresh bread, waiting at heaven's weathered door as sweet, homey aromas drift through the air.

This was the memorable lesson He taught to the ancient Israelites. As they journeyed from slavery in Egypt to a new life in the Promised Land, the Lord gave them fresh bread every morning. Manna, as it was called, contained every vitamin and nutrient they would ever need. It had a sweet, nutty flavor. The psalmist called it "the bread of angels."[3]

This heavenly fresh bread, however, had one other notable property: You couldn't store it up. You couldn't rely on leftovers from yesterday's meal. You had to gather it fresh every day.

> I will rain down bread from heaven for you. The people are to go out each day and gather enough for that day. In this way I will test them and see whether they will follow my instructions.[4]

Some of the stubborn Israelites ignored God's directions. They tried hoarding their divine provisions. Notice what happened when they did:

> Some of them paid no attention to Moses; they kept part of it until morning, but it was full of maggots and began to smell.[5]

In other words, their disobedience became odoriferous and obvious to everyone!

Funny thing about fresh bread: "Fresh" has a time limit. It's like a sweet, beautiful sunrise. You can't loiter and catch it later. It's fresh for the moment. Procrastinate, and it's soon swallowed up by the sunlight that bids you resume your daily busyness and activity.

Have you ever visited a town or church where a great revival once took place—only now it's little more than a musty old museum? The life has gone. The excitement has vanished. The crowds have dwindled to a trickle; the whole place smells of old boards and mildewed carpets. A friend of mine told me about visiting a village in Wales where in 1904 the Welsh Revival had swept across the countryside like a prairie fire. It made him sad to see one of the stone churches erected in that era now being used as a barn—a doorless, windowless husk for storing hay.

That church had once dispensed fresh bread. Now it was full of straw.

For good reason Jesus instructed us to pray, "Give us *each day* our daily bread."[6] The Lord wants us to come to Him *each day* for what we will need on that day. Nowhere does He ask us to pray for our weekly bread, or our monthly bread, or our yearly bread. He fashioned us to need fresh bread daily, and nothing but daily fresh bread will ever satisfy our souls.

BECAUSE LIFE IS SO "DAILY"

Do you know another important reason why we need fresh bread, why we must make it a priority to come every day to learn from the Divine Mentor?

We all have a tendency to drift.

We rarely get lost overnight. We drift along and gradually float off on the waves, usually over a drawn-out period of time. Hearing from God every day has the power to counteract that drifting, as His Word declares: "We must pay more careful attention, therefore, to what we have heard, so that we do not drift away."[7]

How do we do that? How do we "pay more careful attention"? By submitting ourselves every day to the Holy Spirit, our Divine Mentor, asking Him to teach, guide, and correct us.

With each passing day I fear I'm more profoundly ignorant than the day before. Yet the Spirit remains with His remedial student and continues unabated in His attempts to tutor me. It's during these definitive moments in silence before Him that I come to grips with myself. I realize I'm not even remotely ready for life let alone prepared to fulfill His assignment for me.

That's a scary reality but a restorative one. My frequent stops before the mirror of His Word reiterate His power and remind me of my frailty.

Frequent because I quickly forget.

Daily because my soul is usually more connected to self than to the sacred.

Fresh bread. It is the staple of my soul . . . and yours.

STAY NEAR THE DOOR

God wants us to stay near to Him, huddled up in His presence . . . to stay near the door where the fresh bread is dispensed. If we read the Bible only when we have a need, then drifting away is a foregone conclusion. We won't hear from God every day, and so we won't even notice as we begin to float farther and farther away from His Son.

But if we enter the Bible daily and journal the instructions and advice offered us, we gain the wisdom to make a course correction. We need to remain at the bakery door.

Blessed is the man who listens to me, *watching daily* at my doors, waiting at my doorway.[8]

Reading this verse always takes me back to that bakery in Molokai . . . standing under the star-strewn sky waiting for the attendant to poke his head around the weathered door: "What bread would you like, and how much?"

Know this: All of us drift *somewhat,* because we still wear human flesh. We must contend with and abate a warped and sinful nature that will accompany us on our journey throughout this lifetime. However, meeting with divine mentors on a daily basis will allow us to make the necessary corrections *in smaller increments,* so we don't have to go through the shock of a major adjustment. We must make frequent stops. Without consistent compass checks to assure our direction, we can drift and drift and discover too late our miscalculations.

ENTERING THE BIBLE

"Reading the Bible" and "entering the Bible" are two vastly differing experiences. *Reading* the Bible will tell you about history and render facts. *Entering* the Bible will be like shadowing Christ. You'll hear Him speak to a lame man, to a leper, to someone being denounced by a chief priest or an elder. You'll hear the wisdom by which He responds out of full security and absolute confidence. You'll hear what He says to a woman about to be executed. You'll hear what He has to say to those seeking Him or rejecting Him. The more you hear about God and His heart, the more your faith will grow.

"Faith comes from hearing," Paul wrote, "and hearing by the word of Christ."[9] You build your faith as you hear God's Word, and one of the best ways to hear is through *entering the Bible*.

Wisdom is built layer by layer. Like a varnished table, its depth comes from dozens of thin coverings. After each coat has been meticulously applied, the table becomes almost translucent. The depth looks haunting, giving you the illusion that you could reach through and touch the grain of the wood. That kind of transparency and sheen doesn't come with one thick pour but rather through layer upon layer of applied coats.

Wisdom is built in the same way. So is solid character that will stand the tests of time. You can't get a shot or take a pill for it. You grow into it day by day, step by step, word by word. It comes only through consistency, and it yields its deepest gems only to those not in a hurry for a quick fix.

Wisdom is like a muscle, and you don't build muscles overnight.

I thought I could.

When I was in the sixth grade, a friend told me that if you pump weights, your muscles enlarge. So we headed for the gym and began to lift weights with the fervor of Schwarzenegger wannabes. After a morning of furious sets, we stood in front of the mirror, searching for any signs of bulging muscles, eagerly anticipating our renovation. We tried assisting the process by flexing, extending, and poising. We waited . . . and waited.

And I'm still waiting to this day.

Wait *daily* at the weathered door for fresh bread. Gather it *daily* until how you live begins to match what you believe.

HEAVEN'S WONDER BREAD

If you're close to my age, you may remember the old Wonder Bread commercials. Their motto was "Wonder Bread helps kids build strong bodies twelve ways!"

Whether they could substantiate those claims about their white bread made from refined, bleached flour may be up for debate. However, fresh bread from heaven *will* build a strong soul in twelve different ways—at the very least! However, if you were to sniff at it occasionally or just taste it without ever swallowing, it wouldn't help you much. In fact, doing so might give you the illusion of being healthy while you observe opposite results.

INFORMATION

If you take the Word of God into your head and spout it out to others, but you don't take it any further, that's called *information*. The Pharisees were truly remarkable when it came to information, intellectually amassing all kinds of biblical data. But they neglected to apply it. They refused to live it. They never oriented their lives to it—even though they loved to teach it to others.

No wonder Jesus told His followers,

> The teachers of the law and the Pharisees sit in Moses' seat. So you must obey them and do everything they tell you. But do not do what they do, for they do not practice what they preach.[10]

Information alone isn't enough.

INSPIRATION

If you hear an exciting message that makes you want to stand up and shout, but you take it no further, that can be called *inspiration*. Most of us are pretty good at this. We love to listen to stirring music and attend motivating seminars—but usually that's as far as it goes. This makes for good conversation and stirs our intentions, but it leaks. This kind of *inspiration* alone isn't enough.

INCARNATION

Conversely, when you ask, "How will I live differently because of what God has just said to me?" then *incarnation* has begun. Incarnation is what changes the world. Incarnation transforms your family. Incarnation rewrites your future. When God's Word bleeds out your fingertips and toenails—when you treat it as fresh bread, to be consumed daily—that's when it makes you a *disciple*.

- ·· Just in your head: information.
- ·· Just in your heart: inspiration.
- ·· When it bleeds out of you: *incarnation*.

When it's just in your head, it makes you pharisaical. (And inside each one of us is a Pharisee just waiting to grow up!)

When it's just in your heart, it makes you a fanatic.

When it bleeds out your toes, it makes you authentic.

GUARDRAILS

A daily time at the Lord's feet will build guardrails in your character. On the inside, they act like the rumble strips that parallel the sides of highways. Two or three feet from the edge, these small bumps or indentations will cause your veering car to encounter a seismic moment that triggers alert. It can awaken the near-dead! I know by experience.

But if that doesn't do the trick, the highways also have guardrails. Guardrails are a bit more strident in their reprimand of straying drivers, but they can also save your life.

We all need guardrails.

There will be times when we'll basically be on autopilot. Temptation will snare you. Anger will put a stranglehold on you. Depression will take its toll by berating you. You'll be tempted to cash it all in just to dodge the pain, *but* your internal guardrails, formed by God's Word, will keep you from regret. The season will pass, and after the struggle you'll look back and say, "I'm so glad I had guardrails that were stronger than my errant driving!"

ONE NIGHT WITH TEMPTATION

None of us are immune to momentary drifts from wise decision-making. Several years ago, when I was feeling tired and weary, temptation availed itself with a perfect alibi. I'd completed an engagement early and had a free night in a hotel near the airport. I was unaware that this particular area was well known for prostitution.

I asked the maître d' for a table for one. I was no sooner seated than a strikingly beautiful woman sat down across from me.

"Are you satisfied with this hotel?" she asked. I assumed she was a hotel representative surveying the customers.

"Why, absolutely," I replied. "This is a beautiful hotel."

"And the rooms? Are they to your satisfaction?"

"Oh, yes," I said naïvely. "The beds are so comfy!"

"I am here to offer you elite services," she continued, "reserved only for gentlemen."

I must be pretty dim, because I still didn't catch on. "Services?" I asked.

"Yes, escort services that will make your stay a memorable one."

It finally clicked, and my light went from dim to bright. She was working, all right, but not as a surveyor.

Immediately an inner voice interrupted. *No one would know,* cajoled the passing ruse. *You're in a strange hotel, in a strange part of the country . . . and you deserve a break today!*

It may have been an illusion, but I thought I saw, out the corner of my eye, Joseph running from Potiphar's wife. And when he passed me, he yelled, "You'd better follow me, Cordeiro—and follow me *now*!"

"Excuse me," I said. "I forgot something in my room." And I ran to catch Joseph.

When I got to my room, I bolted the door, and to this day I'm so glad I did!

Where do those parameters come from? Where do you get them?

From the men and women who've been there before you.

- •• Joseph had to flee Potiphar's wife. He knew lust's pull. (So did Samson.)
- •• Abigail had to deal with David's anger as well as her own frustration. She dealt wisely; her example will guard you from costly mistakes.
- •• Elijah's depression found him alone in desperation. Jeremiah knew about it too; they'll both take the time to teach you.
- •• Peter left his calling to go back to fishing. He knew about the feeling of giving up. He has so much to share.

So where did you get the guardrails? You incorporated them into your soul when you ate the fresh bread.

Inside Activity

// SCRIPTURE

Saul was very angry. . . . "They have credited David with tens of thousands," he thought, "but me with only thousands. What more can he get but the kingdom?" And from that time on Saul kept a jealous eye on David. The next day an evil spirit from God came forcefully upon Saul. (1 Samuel 18:8–10 NIV)

// OBSERVATION

Make no mistake about it: Heaven and hell watch *inside activity* more than outside activity. Although inside activity is not immediately visible, that doesn't mean it can't be instantly toxic. Such was the case with Saul's envy of David. Its lethal poison lay silently in the king's heart . . . until the songs began.

// APPLICATION

This is the litmus test for any leader: He's tested not by what he does as much as by how he responds to what others do.

- • When others' successes are greater than yours, do you rejoice or are you secretly bothered?
- • When a peer or a competitor flops in performance, do you secretly rejoice or do you genuinely weep?

"God sees not as man sees, for man looks at the outward appearance, but the Lord looks at the heart" (1 Samuel 16:7).

Inside activity is something heaven and hell watch for. Letting inside activity go unchecked will cause our hearts to become septic, and the forces of hell will respond with oppressive results. Our motives get skewed; thinking we are righteous, we become foolish and deceived.

I need to check my inside activity often. I must monitor my heart and my thoughts. What's taking up my mind's time and my inner conversation? Heaven monitors my inside activity to determine my strength.

So does hell.

// PRAYER

Search me, O God, and know my heart. Try me and see if there is any wicked way in me, and lead me in Your everlasting way! (See Psalm 139:23–24.)

STARVING IN A LAND OF PLENTY

There's a famine in the church today. It's not always so easy to spot, though, because we tend to see with the wrong set of eyes. One of our more neglected mentors, the prophet Amos, told us long ago about the coming famine:

> "Behold, days are coming," declares the Lord God, "when I will send a famine on the land, not a famine for bread or a thirst for water, but rather for *hearing the words of the Lord*."[11]

Today's church suffers from a famine of fresh bread—the Bread of Life—and it's not from a dearth of resources. A recent Barna Report says Americans spent fifty-nine *billion* dollars last year on Christian products and programs. No shortage there! We have a plethora of events and books, seminars and DVDs, each promising a magical elixir—everything from personal growth to financial freedom to absolute fulfillment to global revival.

We have prepackaged antidotes to small-group woes, motivational messages to stir the soul, and conferences that guarantee congregational growth. Books advertise prayers that will negate your future ills. Music guarantees to send your spirit soaring. Plug-and-play ministries are packaged in boxed sets to increase church attendance. And Scripture wristbands provide conscience-soothing assurance of whose army we're in (without mandating the time or expense of appropriate spiritual training).

Despite all this, few would deny the spiritual famine raging across our land. If we're going to fulfill the Lord's calling for our lives, we'll need to be better nourished and in sharper condition. Placebos—sugar-coated spiritual boosters—may give us the taste of sweetness, but they will never strengthen us adequately to vanquish our foes. They will never grow us to be pillars and supports of the truth that will be required in these last days. They will never deliver the necessary character to the young leaders called to take us into the future.

We must tap into the same Source that nourished the saints of old. Like Isaac, who dug again the wells of his father, Abraham, so too we must "dig again" the wells of our fathers, so that we might journey through the deserts to see God's promises fulfilled.

Do you long to see the Spirit of the Lord work within you? Do you desire to reflect His heart more than your own? If so, I have just one piece of advice for you:

Eat fresh bread.

Wait every day by heaven's door. Get bread while it's warm and fragrant, fresh from the oven. No matter how early you have to get up or how late you have to stay up to find such bread, it will be well worth your time and effort.

HOW
SWEET
THAT
VOICE!

9

Oak All the Way to the Core

Blessed is the man who trusts in the Lord, whose confidence is in him. He will be like a tree planted by the water that sends out its roots by the stream. It does not fear when heat comes; its leaves are always green. It has no worries in a year of drought and never fails to bear fruit.[1]

We live in a veneer world, one in which *image* is often valued more than *reality*, reputation more than character, and perception more than actuality. Veneer looks enough like the real thing, and it costs less.

But the image facade lasts only until the next latest style rolls off the assembly line. Image, again and again and again, demands that we forget the old and crave the new.

Nevertheless, when it comes to the substance life is made of, veneer is not enough. Success without regret, as well as healthy families and fruitful churches, require credibility and veracity. For God's presence to be in attendance, it has to be genuine all the way to the core.

HEIRLOOM TREASURES AND HEIR-HEAD CONSUMERS

Anna and I had just moved into our first home. Needing a desk, I stopped by a furniture store. My dream was to own a genuine oak rolltop desk . . . and there one was, right in front of me! I loved the nostalgic look. I thought of how it would make a wonderful treasure to pass down to my grandchildren someday. It was on sale, so I threw caution to the wind and bought it.

I was proud of this stately piece of history that my grandchildren would one day inherit and call "Grandpa's desk from the turn of the century." I was feeling quite smug about my purchase until one day I noticed something curious. Upon closer inspection, I was horrified to find that the only genuine oak on the whole desk were the rolls of the rolltop. The rest was oak veneer covering pressboard innards. I'd been too quick on the draw. I had purchased a pressboard desk that I thought was solid oak!

No one would want a pressboard desk as a family heirloom. If it's going to be valuable and treasured, it has to be authentic and genuine. That alone would bring the worth we esteem. It has to be oak all the way to the core.

Do you know the same could be said of character? We are generally one of two types: veneer or solid oak. Under ideal circumstances both look identical. You could easily mistake veneer for the real deal. But when life delivers its inevitable rough and tumble, it instantly becomes evident what's made of sawdust and glue and what's oak all the way through.

What's your choice? They look alike on the surface, but one is a cheap imitation and one is eternal.

MAKE IT SYSTEMIC

These days the world is crying out for the genuine article. To meet the need, we can't be made of religious-looking veneer covering pressboard. We all know, however, that what we espouse and who we are can be two different people. Often what we are under the spotlight is not who we are in the shadows.

Things were different with Jesus. Even His enemies looked at Him and exclaimed, "Who *is* this that speaks with such authority? And where did He *get* this authority?" Do you know where He got it? He allowed the seed of the Word to enter and reach deeply into His core being. The result: a systemic accumulation and application of wisdom.

Jesus' authority was commensurate with his congruency: *What He said was who He was.*

For us, here's where it all begins to come together. A daily time at the feet of Jesus causes a metamorphosis of authenticity. His Word on a daily basis identifies the pressboard sectors of our thinking and decision-making; somehow the alchemy of the Scriptures exchanges the false for the genuine. It happens slowly, over time. It is an imperceptible transformation that requires daily exposure to His Word. But as you spend that consistent time in the Word, the Divine Mentor will make sure your oak structure is more than a thin exterior. He'll take it right to the core of your being.

THE WALL

In Hawaii, thirty-two thousand runners participate each year in the Honolulu Marathon. They come from virtually every nation in the world, but the lion's share comes from Japan. They arrive by the planeload. Young and old, men and women, ready or not, they converge to explore, step by step, 26.2 miles of Oahu. The morning of the race, they look die-cut: streamlined running shoes, running outfits, and number patches. Some arrive expecting a leisurely stroll, some look forward to the challenge, but the true marathoners will be separated from the novices at . . . *the wall.*

Though invisible, you can't miss it. Around eighteen miles from the shot of the starter's pistol, it pounces on you. Every step past "the wall" feels like someone is driving a hot poker through each thigh. Your shoes are on fire, and the road starts to punch back.

Every runner hits the wall, but how hard that wall feels will depend entirely on his preparation before the race.

Some run right through the wall with only a modicum of fatigue and pain. Others slam into the wall and fall back in a daze.

What makes the difference? Is it the wall itself? No, the wall exists for the elite and the novitiate. The solidity of the wall is determined by what the runners have *in them* when they hit it.

Veneer falls short or falls apart. Oak has what it takes to finish and finish well.

THE FRUIT OF DAILY DEVOTIONS

A daily exposure to the Lord's heart and ways begins a transformation process. We begin to diminish; He increases. But that's the process of authenticity. It comes slowly. Veneer you can make quickly. Real oak takes time to grow.

It begins deep in our hearts, in our inner man. He tutors us, and He renews our souls with a trickle charge, not an overnight blast. "Be still," He says, "and know that I am God."[2] You can catch a glimpse of Him in a crowd, but you get to know Him best in the stillness.

KNOWING HIM BETTER

> One who looks intently *at the perfect law, the law of liberty, and abides by it, not having become a forgetful hearer but an effectual doer, this man will be blessed in what he does.*[3]

There are many speed-reading courses for the active businessperson. They can help you scan pages in a flash, and they promise to guide you through an entire book in one sitting. I have another course to offer, another alternative: It's called the Slow-Reading Course for Serious Disciples.

James is a primary sponsor.

James was one of Jesus' half brothers. James didn't believe that Jesus was the Messiah until after the resurrection, but when he became a believer, he caught fire! He was so convinced that he became a powerful witness of Christ's transforming power. History tells us his devotion was so genuine that he would spend hours a day in prayer. People nicknamed him "Camel Knees" because of the calluses that formed from hours of prayer.

Of the Word, James says in effect: "Look intently. There's far too much to apprehend in one sitting. Look *intently*."

The word *intently* comes from a term that means "to stoop to take a closer look." This is the posture of a curious student, a student intent on learning.

"Intention" is when transformation happens.

> "I have not spoken in secret, from somewhere in a land of darkness; I have not said to Jacob's descendants, 'Seek me in vain.' I, the Lord, speak the truth; I declare what is right."[4]

God isn't inaccessible. He's neither coy nor introverted. But He does require us to seek Him. This hones our hearts and purifies our motives. And the ancillary benefits are manifold. Seeking and searching for God builds our faith, like pecking out of the shell strengthens a newborn chick.

> "You will seek me and find me when you seek me with all your heart. I will be found by you," declares the Lord.[5]

CREATIVE AFFINITY

The more you know Him, the more you love Him, and the more you love Him, the more you will want to know Him.

Why is knowing Him so important to God? Why does He want us to love Him with ever-increasing devotion? It's because of something called "creative affinity." Creative affinity means you become increasingly more like that which you love the most. You take on the characteristics of whom or what you cherish most deeply.

Have you ever noticed that when a couple has been married fifty or sixty years they start to look alike? *People start to resemble what they love.*

Hawaii is famous for its beautiful beaches and air-brushed waves. Surfing is a commonly loved sport, and a friend of mine is addicted. He constantly reads surf magazines, has surf posters plastered on his walls, and dresses in surfing attire. Everything about him shouts, "Surf's up!" He looks like a surfboard, talks like a surfer, and smells like seaweed.

I have another friend who's passionate about tennis. He couldn't care less about surfing, but he constantly reads tennis magazines, sports a haircut that resembles a tennis ball, and spends all his spare time on the court. Tennis is his passion, and believe me, it shows.

This is why the greatest commandment of all is to "love the Lord your God with all your heart, with all your soul, and with all your mind, and with all your strength."[6] The more we love God, the more we become the people He created us to be.

FREE AT LAST!

The more you know God's Word, the more freedom comes into your life. That's why Jesus said, "You will *know* the truth, and the truth will set you free."[7]

What will set you free is not *only* the truth: It's the truth you *know* that will set you free. If you don't know the truth—if it remains imprisoned in the pages of Scripture—it will not free you. The truth alone is wonderful, but until you know it and walk by its light, freedom will always remain ethereal and out of reach.

There isn't anything we can do or say that will make the truth less true. It's true no matter how or what we think about it. But if we have not come to know its power and its applicability, we will still be in bondage to old thinking and perspectives. In other words, if you want the truth to free you, you cannot allow it to remain undiscovered. Grab a pick and start mining!

FREE TO GO!

"But," some will say, "the Bible is full of do's and don'ts! Doesn't this mean that the more you know it, the more bound up you'll be?"

Some time ago I was late in leaving for a hospital visit. I knew I'd need to hurry to arrive in time for visiting hours, but I got caught behind a slow driver in the right lane. I had to stay behind her, since I needed to turn right at the next street. As we approached the turn, it became obvious she was going to turn right too. But as the light turned yellow, she stopped.

In Hawaii, you can turn right on a red light if you first stop to make sure the road is clear. Since I didn't see a "Right Turn Only on Arrow" sign, and since there were no cars or pedestrians, I expected her to turn.

But instead she sat there. I dislike it when people honk at me, so I refrain from prodding someone else with my horn. So—honorably and considerately—I yelled at her from the confines of my car: "Lady, move! . . . Maybe this week?"

Still she remained in a state of suspended animation.

Finally the light turned green and she prodded her car forward. I careened around the corner, and as I passed her I complained, *If you would just read your driver's manual, you'd realize you could have turned!*

At that moment I realized an eternal truth. Knowing the law frees you up. NOT knowing it will bind you up! The more we get to know God and His Word, the freer we will be. We'll have a new and ever-growing confidence, and where our lives normally would stop or stall out, we'll be able to go forward.

I don't know that driver, or her name, but I bless her for giving me the opportunity to catch that insight.

THE JOY OF OBEDIENCE

> Loving God means keeping his commandments, and his commandments are not burdensome.[8]

One of the main barometers of my love for God is whether or not obeying Him is becoming increasingly more difficult . . . or increasingly more joyful. Many believe that keeping God's commandments is an arduous, difficult, unpleasant task, like slogging through ankle-deep sludge in a cold rainstorm.

That's the opposite of what John says! If the Lord's requirements seem tough for me, then I have to revisit the cross of Christ and His sacrifice of compassion for me. When I catch a fresh glimpse of His stunning love and grace, my problems shrink. The greater the love, the less my sacrifice seems.

Laws in America that seem obvious are: One must not murder family members, abandon children in a strange city, or throw an electrically connected appliance into the bathtub while a spouse is in it.

These are admirable statutes that I have no problem keeping. Why would that be? They aren't burdensome because I love my family. I love my children and I love my spouse. I would never want to injure them or bring harm to them in any way, so the laws mandating that I treat them well aren't difficult. The deeper the love, the more joyful the obedience.

But what happens if my love for my family diminishes? There's the difference. Laws regarding how they should be treated become tougher to obey.

THE BEGINNING OF THE MIRACULOUS

One of the greatest gifts you'll receive from entering the Bible on a daily basis is *an increasing resistance to offense*. Don't miss this! Taking offense, justified or unjustified, will impede the miraculous in your life.

We see this played out in Mark's gospel. When Jesus stood up to teach in the synagogue, the people's response to Him was sketchy at best. We find these words: "'Is not this the carpenter, the son of Mary, and brother of James and Joses and Judas and Simon? Are not his sisters here with us?' And they took *offense* at Him.'"[9]

Mark then shows the results of taking up an offense: "And *He could do no miracle there* except that He laid His hands on a few sick people and healed them.'"[10]

It is not that Jesus didn't *want* to. "He *could do no miracle* there. . . ." This has always intrigued me. Here's the lesson: We can either take hold of an offense—which results in letting go of the miraculous—or we can let go of an offense in order to take hold of the miraculous.

The choice is ours.

Great peace have they which *love Thy Law:* and nothing shall offend them.[11]

A special dose of peace is granted to those who love God's Word; they will develop a greater resilience to offense.

In my life, I desperately need to make room for more miracles. Therefore, I cannot afford to be offended—I cannot grant myself the option of taking offense.

There *will* be many occasions where you can easily and naturally take offense: Your advice is not taken. You're inexplicably passed over for a promotion. You're marginalized by your coworkers. You're not invited to a luncheon.

If anyone had the right to be offended, it was Jesus. Chased by demons, plotted against by religious leaders, stalked by lepers, deserted by His own disciples. Yet we find in Isaiah these words foreshadowing the Messiah's character:

> He will not be disheartened or crushed until He has established justice in the earth.[12]

And the source of that inner strength? A love for God's Word.

Never underestimate it. It just may be the beginning of the miraculous in your life.

LOVING GOD'S WORD

An ever-increasing love for God's Word develops with consistent exposure. His Word contains a proven chemistry that ignites the causal heart and deepens our yearning for His next instructions. David weighs in on this when he says, "As the deer pants for the water brooks, so my soul pants for You, O God."[13]

I *so* look forward to my daily devotions. In fact, I can't wait to get up in the morning. As I lie in bed, sometimes I stare at the clock next to my bed, waiting for the alarm's cantankerous sound. As soon as it complains, I get excited. I head to the nearest café, order a cup of steaming coffee and a scone, open my Bible, and I'm in heaven. I look forward to entering the Word and talking with the likes of Shadrach, Meshach, and Abednego in ancient Iraq, facing not the terrorism of al-Qaeda but an equally perilous foe, Nebuchadnezzar and his fiery furnace.

I need to hear God's instructions for today. You see, the Holy Spirit knows what challenges I will be facing, and He is ready to deposit the wisdom necessary for every situation. I just need to press in to hear His direction.

Several years ago I wrote a little journal entry to my son, Aaron.

Dear Aaron,

Today I'm speaking at a youth conference. Earlier today while I was tuning my acoustic Martin guitar, the soundman cranked up some ear-piercing rock music, the kind that makes you feel your heart beat with each thump of the kick drum. I kept trying to tune my guitar by putting my ear closer and closer to it, but to no avail. My guitar was no match for the high-powered speakers. We didn't have digital tuners, so I had to do it the old-fashioned way . . . by listening. I put my ear right onto the wood itself. And then, lo and behold, regardless of how loud the music raged, I could still hear my acoustic guitar. But it wasn't because my guitar got any louder. It was because my ear got closer.

Aaron, you'll come to times when voices around you will be so loud that it will be difficult to hear the gentle voice of our Savior. Yes, He can speak in thunderous ways too. But that wouldn't require any faith to hear Him, would it? God will always be speaking. But sometimes in order to hear Him, we've got to bend our ears so that we will hear the very vibrations of His heart.

And Aaron, don't just pretend to know Him. Take the time to really know Him by listening to His heart. And I think that is what really pleases God anyway. Doesn't it? He doesn't want us to expect His voice always to be loud and booming. Instead, He wants us to be a people who are willing simply to bend our ears to touch Him. What pleases Him most are people who are willing to take time to listen every day. Develop ears that hear.

—Dad

Hear from God every day. You will notice how making positive changes becomes less and less difficult. And you will observe how the plasticized veneer progressively falls away, revealing the growing oak underneath.

Not an Overnight Wonder

Once again, you don't become oak all the way to the core overnight. It doesn't happen in a flash of insight or a wave of emotion. This growth takes place gradually. It eventuates over time as we cooperate with the counsel we receive from those who have gone before us.

Shedding veneer in exchange for solid oak is possible. I'm sure of this because of what happened to Naaman. You can watch his story unfold in 2 Kings 5.

Naaman was a commander in the Aramean army. He was also a leper. It was reported to him that a certain Israelite prophet, Elisha, would pray for people and that God would actually heal them. Arameans had no dealings with the Israelites, but, nevertheless, desperate Naaman stemmed his pride and made the long trek, reaching Israel only to find the prophet refusing to grant an audience. Instead, Naaman was sent to the Jordan River to dip himself seven times in its muddy waters.

The humiliated commander was furious. Fortunately, his servant, Gehazi, said, "If he had asked you to accomplish a near impossible task in order to gain your healing, would you have done it? He is simply asking you to do something easily attainable. Isn't it worth a try?"[14]

With that, Naaman hitched up his pants and promptly waded in. He dipped his afflicted body under the current, and with each completed dunk something of him drifted downstream . . . a little of his pride.

Every time Naaman's head broke the water, God broke down his conceit. By the seventh dip, the work in him was completed. His self-consciousness and smug self-will had been dissolved by the water and the hand of God. He was now positioned for healing.

God is intimately acquainted with our ways, and He's more concerned about *transformation* than *information*. Our daily times in the Word are not necessarily designed to produce theologians. The primary purpose is to produce *disciples*. When we enter the Bible, we don't enter to study it as much as we allow it to study us!

LIVING WITH INTEGRITY

> There is no creature hidden from His sight, but all things are open and laid bare to the eyes of Him with whom we have to do.[15]

I love the Bible because it fillets my heart.

Just like you, I'm a person with a propensity to go in the wrong direction. We need the Word of God and its mentors to keep us on track. Hebrews 4:12 says that the Word of God is living and active, sharper than any two-edged sword, able to divide between the soul and spirit, discerning my thoughts and my intentions.

When I read the Bible, God's Spirit pierces deeply—nothing is hidden, all things are laid bare. God extensively examines what's driving my desires and thoroughly inspects my intentions.

When I enter the Bible, it reads me as much as I read it! I'm actually submitting myself to a panel of mentors—standing before a benevolent tribunal tasked with checking my motives. Each time we read God's Word, the motives of our heart are scoured and cleared of toxic intrusion. I know that if I want to finish my race without being disqualified, I need that kind of genuine integrity.

A good friend of mine once wrote:

> Search me, O God, and know my heart;
> Try me and know my anxious thoughts;
> And see if there be any hurtful way in me,
> And lead me in the everlasting way.[16]

David loved God intensely, and he knew that without God's pleasure he'd be on an uphill slope. He didn't want the slightest shadow of sin to come between him and the Lord. In later years he would ask a question he himself would answer:

How can a young man keep his way pure?
By keeping it according to Your word. . . .
Your word have I treasured in my heart,
That I may not sin against You.[17]

"You Are a Dead Man"

Genesis 20 narrates a peculiar encounter between the chosen patriarch Abraham and the pagan ruler Abimelech. It wasn't one of Abraham's finer moments. Passing through Philistine territory was perilous at best; it was exponentially more difficult with a beautiful wife.

In those days it was commonly accepted that a king had every right to take a single woman to be his wife or concubine. If the woman were beautiful and married, the king could simply kill the husband and thereby make the beauty "single."

To save his own hide, Abraham told the king that his wife, Sarah, was his sister. Abimelech, in short order, had Sarah delivered to his palace. He would meet his soon-to-be bride the following morning.

But that very night God said to Abimelech in a dream, "You are a dead man."[18]

In effect, the conversation went like this:

"Why?" Abimelech answered. "What have I done?"

"You have taken another man's wife," God said.

"Didn't Abraham say to me, 'She is my sister'?" he pleaded. And then he added, "In the *integrity of my heart* and the innocence of my hands I have done this."[19]

"Then God said to him in the dream, 'Yes, I know that in the integrity of your heart you have done this, and I also kept you from sinning against Me.'"[20]

Integrity is recognizable to God!

When we are faithful to let God's Word scrub our hearts, He provides us with divine protection. As our hearts are laid bare before the Word, He points out any wrong motives we may have.

REMOVING THE UNSEEN

But it doesn't end there. God told Abimelech, "Restore the man's wife [to her husband]."[21] And then the Word says this: "For the Lord had closed fast all the wombs of the household of Abimelech because of Sarah, Abraham's wife."[22]

The Philistines had no idea every womb in their land had been shut. It might have been a few years before they would have recognized they were dying off as a people due to an utter barrenness. In one generation they would have been annihilated. But God reopened their wombs *before* the consequences of infertility became widespread.

In a similar way, there are times in our lives where sin is in motion and the consequences are in process . . . and God intercepts, arresting the course of sin. When we allow Him to scour our hearts in order to bring about integrity, He can rescind the natural course of sin's consequences—and we may never know anything about it until we're safely on the other side!

Do you want to succeed in life and in ministry? Become a person of integrity. Allow God to cleanse your heart through His Word. In fact, one of the greatest things you can do for yourself is to make sure your heart's hub is one of genuine integrity, clear to the core. That will be your greatest legacy— your only legacy.

THE FASTEST SETTING IS ON SLOW

The Lord is not slow in keeping his promise, as some understand slowness. He is patient with you, not wanting anyone to perish, but everyone to come to repentance.[23]

Here's a new definition for "slowness": *God's optimum speed in bringing about His likeness in you.* This is especially important to remember whenever we start to worry about how long our transformation seems to be taking.

You might call it "slow," but God calls it "just right."

It requires patience. Not yours . . . His!

And the reason He's so patient with us is that He doesn't want us to perish. Like Naaman the leper, we need time to come to repentance. We require days, sometimes seasons, to change our mind and direction.

A hurry-up father once approached future U.S. president James A. Garfield while he was still the president of a local college: "Is there any way you can get my son through this institution faster than four years?" he implored. "Time is running short, and the business world is waiting!"

"It all depends on what you want," Garfield wisely replied. "Squash will take only three months, but if you want oak, that requires four years."

You can manufacture veneer, but you grow oak. It will take a bit longer, but that's the only way to be authentic . . . clear to the core.

Marching Orders

// SCRIPTURE

What I tell you in the darkness, speak in the light; and
what you hear whispered in your ear, proclaim upon
the housetops. (Matthew 10:27)

// OBSERVATION

The question is not "Is God speaking?" The question is "Am I listening?" Oh, God can thunder, if He so chooses, but I think He'd rather whisper. That way, my heart has to incline toward Him. He speaks in the darkness and whispers in my ear. If I'm not listening to Him in the darkness, what will I speak when I get into the light? If I'm not hearing Him whisper in my ear, what will I have to proclaim on the housetops?

// APPLICATION

What a great word! I am duly reminded today not only to talk to God in prayer; it is equally important for me to *hear* Him in prayer! He is constantly giving me words of instruction for my marriage, ministry, and future. I cannot afford not to incline my ear to Him and listen for His whispers.

// PRAYER

Dear Jesus, help me to hear You today. I want to be still so that I may hear Your marching orders for my day, my week, my life. Speak, Lord. Your servant is listening!

10

Where the Rubber Meets the Road

When he sits on the throne as king, he must copy
for himself this body of instruction . . . and read it
daily as long as he lives.[1]

N ow, at last, comes the interactive part. Here is where
we start expanding and including others. Among
believers, there's no greater way to deepen one
another's faith than through reading the Scriptures together.

THE 20/20/20 PROGRAM

This is the place at which we dive into the nuts and bolts of
what it takes to build genuine disciples. We've all heard the
term *20/20*, which usually refers to great vision. To make the
journaling process unique and easier to remember, we've established a *20/20/20*, which refers to a way to achieve superior spiritual vision.

Very simply, here's what you do:

•• For twenty minutes, read the portion of God's Word according to the reading schedule for that day. It will take an average reader about that long to cover the bases.

•• For the next twenty minutes, take *one* Scripture that the Holy Spirit has highlighted for you and journal on it, using the SOAP method. This is not a time to play theologian. From the chapters you've read, choose only one Scripture. Even if several catch your attention, select one thing the Spirit is bringing to your attention. Write your thoughts out in manuscript form using standard grammar. No notations or CliffsNotes. Take the time to explain it clearly. Writing this way will help you to be exact in your thinking and clear in your understanding.

•• During the final twenty minutes, have the group share, one person at a time, what each person has journaled. Everyone takes a turn. No preaching allowed, and no special offerings allowed. Just read the entry. Discuss what you've heard in an easygoing and encouraging way. When you listen to others share their journals, you'll draw from their wisdom and insights.

THE LIFE GROUP

I meet with four groups weekly whenever I'm in town. (We hold "Life Groups" attended by as few as two and as many as twenty-two.) There are times when I do my devotions in solitude, of course, but I am not impeded in the least when I do them in groups. After all, for the first forty minutes, no one talks anyway! We're all listening to those whom God is using in the Bible to instruct us. Everyone's reading for twenty minutes and then journaling for twenty minutes, so it's *quiet.* You always do your reading and journaling in the quiet, so, in effect, during that part of the time you're still shut in alone with the Lord.

Only in the last twenty minutes does anyone in the room talk. (For the other forty minutes, the voices come out of the

Word.) Then you have the reward of sharing what you heard from God *and* discovering what He's shown the others in your group. It's simply wonderful!

In the past, when people asked me to mentor them, I usually said, "I'm sorry, but I really don't have the time." Things have changed. Today, when someone asks me for mentoring, I have a very different response.

"Absolutely!"

"*Really*? When?"

"Six-thirty A.M. At the corner café on Mondays; at the office conference room on Tuesdays; right here on Wednesdays; and at the café on Thursdays. Take your pick. Just bring five things: Bible, pen, journal, reading plan, and daily planner. Six-thirty sharp . . . and remember, that's A.M. not P.M."

I always have to add the "A.M. not P.M." because one early evening my wife and I were on our way to dinner, and as we passed by a local café a young Bible college student waved me down. "It's here, right?" he said excitedly.

"Here for what?" I asked.

"The life group! I even brought my five things with me."

I laughed and asked him to return the next Monday *morning* (not evening) at six-thirty. I gently chided him and told him he wasn't late—he was just a week early.

A HOST FOR DISCIPLING

If you were to count up all the people I get to disciple in this way over one week, it comes to eighty-two. And the beautiful thing about it is I've been doing this for twenty years; we've planted nearly a hundred churches at an average of six hundred people in each, and *it all began around life groups*. I don't prepare anything ahead of time except my heart.

The Holy Spirit always will be our special instructor. I just facilitate the session. My goal is not to clone myself. I don't want people necessarily to become like me. I only want them to tap into the same Source I tap into; then they will become who God wants them to be.

We have no interest in duplicating each other. I teach people to sit at the feet of Jesus and hear the Lord's voice for themselves. Doing this will change your life as it does theirs.

Here's an excerpt from a letter I received recently:

Dear Wayne:

You spoke at a conference in our city almost three years ago. At that conference you gave out the Life Journal. I started there in my motel room. I have hardly missed a day in nearly three years. We now have many people in our church who are also journaling and loving it as much as I am. It has changed my life. I have been a pastor for twenty-three years and always have been lacking in discipline. Your encouragement has literally changed my life. I have people commenting that I am a better pastor and my preaching is better—most of them know it is from the journaling.

PICK A PUBLIC SPOT

Usually we meet in public places, like a coffee shop or a little café. When some people hear this, they ask, "Why meet in a coffee shop? Isn't that a little distracting?"

In fact, in my experience, it hasn't been distracting at all. As much as possible, I meet with small groups out in public, not to show off, but because it's always easier to develop a good habit by connecting it with something else you already enjoy. In this way the habit develops much more quickly.

You probably already know why I like to meet in coffee shops. I admit it: I'm a coffee addict. When I get a good cup of coffee and a scone, I'm euphoric. And when I add in my Bible reading . . . well, it's absolute paradise. (That I live in Hawaii doesn't hurt either.)

But there's also another reason I like to meet for devotions in public places. Think of how many people pass by us as they wait in line for their morning coffee. Most will definitely notice five or six people with their Bibles open, writing in journals. Our favorite meeting place is busy; approximately a hundred people will saunter by us in an hour.

Now, let's do the math. Four days a week at a hundred a day . . . that's four hundred people, weekly, moseying past our group, noticing open Bibles and eager disciples. In four weeks 1,600 people will amble by our quiet 20/20/20 testimony.

Over a year, that's almost 21,000 people! Granted, some will be repeat customers.

Here's the important question: How many of the 21,000 passersby will see the open Bibles—and to how many of those will God gently speak? People who are struggling with their marriage may muse, "If I'd been doing that, maybe I wouldn't be in the fix I'm in now." Others with financial difficulties or stuck in a quagmire—God might use the experience to softly draw them to himself.

Thousands and thousands of opportunities for Christ.

Can you think of anything better as you silently seek His face? Thousands and thousands of seeds for the harvest are planted as you sit with divine mentors recounting to you their stories and lessons.

As with Mary, sitting at the Lord's feet and listening to His Word, your daily appointment can allow God to use your little group to touch the lives of untold souls.

And it doesn't stop there. If you were to add up all the "life groups" from across the church, it's staggering. *We can reach our city by having a revival of God's Word!*

Develop the habit of meeting with others to do your devotions, preferably in an appropriate, suitable public place. You'll be surprised about how far reaching an impact it can have.

HOW BIG CAN IT BE?

Some people ask, "What do you do when you have more than five or six people? Can you have a life group of twenty?

And if you do, how can they all share from their journals in just twenty minutes?"

When you have a group larger than five or six, divide up the sharing into smaller groups—threes or fours. That's a lot less intimidating, anyway. If you're in a group of three and someone shares an entry that's a bit off kilter theologically, it probably doesn't feel as traumatic to be lovingly corrected as it would in, say, a group of twenty.

"Iron sharpens iron, so one man sharpens another."[2] I make it a point, constantly, to encourage the young believers in the group. I also use opportunities to applaud where applause is warranted, as well as fix where some fixing is needed!

Peers who have learned to correct and encourage one another create a beautiful atmosphere. I like the *King James* rendering of Romans 15:14, which says, "I myself also am persuaded of you, my brethren, that ye also are full of goodness, filled with all knowledge, able also to admonish one another." These life groups allow us this privilege, to be able to give input and admonishment without devastating one another.

LET IT GROW WILD

I've always loved Oregon in the summer. (Winters are another story.) Riding my motorcycle over the McKenzie Pass has never failed to exhilarate my soul. The scent of the cedars that greet me along the winding roads, the intermittent sights of the mighty McKenzie . . . my windshield turns into a movie screen that features the beautiful verdant forests of Central Oregon.

But one of the most beautiful sights of all is fertile mountains bedecked with splashes of wildflowers. No rigid patterns. No formalized plantings. No categorized species. The beauty is in the green being absolutely splattered with pastel colors choreographed by nature.

Defining "Promotion"

Not from the east, nor from the west, nor from the desert comes [promotion]; but God is the Judge; He puts down one and exalts another. (Psalm 75:6 7)

// OBSERVATION

Promotion. A lovely word to the ears of many because it often means more . . . well, you fill in the blank—cars, clothes . . . things! The blank is not usually filled in with *responsibility* or *work*.

We tend to think anything that brings in more money brings more happiness, satisfaction, and contentment, but that's where the myth begins. A promotion, if not measured correctly, can actually end up stealing my time, my family, my ministry assignment, and even my future. It may require more time away from home or less time for God.

A correctly defined promotion means "another step closer to fulfilling my calling" or "being better able to use my gifts."

// APPLICATION

Don't be fooled into thinking that every "opportunity" is from God. If it's just more money I want, then the devil can accommodate me. (Think of the "promotions" he offered to Jesus—see Luke 4.) If *promotion* means another step away from what's most valuable—even if it comes with a million dollars—don't take it!

Nevertheless, the Lord truly does give promotions. His promotions bring you a step closer to His best, even when not attended by money. The most important element in His promotion is that it will be attended by His blessings. No matter what else, this will make you rich in a way that money never could.

// PRAYER

Thank You, Father, for always helping me define things correctly. Otherwise, I could construe anything that includes *more money* as coming "from You." You have said that every plant You didn't plant will be uprooted (Matthew 15:13). Please help me to be certain that whatever I receive is not a plant from anywhere but from You!

Life groups are like that.

They remind me of flowering ground cover, the low-lying foliage that paints the countryside's crags and imperfections with the softness of grace. The Lord spreads them like stardust until the hills sparkle with crayon colors and springtime hues.

For a season, some will thrive while others give way to new undergrowth. Undiscovered beauties, lying just beneath the surface, explode into the sunlight as fresh rains bid them rise.

SIGNALING THE END OF A FAMINE

As we have seen, the prophet Amos spoke of a coming famine throughout the earth: "Not a famine for bread or a thirst for water, but rather for hearing the words of the Lord."[3]

It's time we break that famine, and in many places the breaking has already begun. Whole denominations are starting to adopt the life group approach. For example, some leaders from United Methodist churches and the Salvation Army have joined the fight against this famine. Baptists, Wesleyans, Charismatics, and Lutherans are doing the same. It's time for the church to rise again in all her beauty.

So let them grow like wildflowers! That's where the splendor will be seen.

CULTIVATE A CULTURE

In our recent book *Culture Shift*,[4] we speak about every church having a culture. It may not be the one we want, but every church has one. In order to develop the right environment, that culture must first be identified and agreed upon.

Early on at New Hope, we decided that one distinctive of our church's culture would be an undying devotion to God and His Word. This has become one of New Hope's strongest tenets in our short history of twelve years.

When you make daily group devotions your custom, you'll be surprised at how quickly it strengthens the culture. And age doesn't matter! Even our elementary students are doing this with a pared-down *Children's Journal;* our junior high students are doing it with the *First Steps Journal.*

When you get people from various age groups meeting to read the Word and to journal, you soon start developing a powerful culture that becomes a silent megaphone, unheralded but unmistakably present.

My goal is to continue developing a culture of undying devotion to God and His Word and to keep on cultivating until it becomes systemic throughout the church.

Be sure to understand one aspect of utmost importance: Doing devotions is not a program! It is a culture, an environment, a shared DNA. Journaling begins with the leaders. When leaders develop a habit, a culture soon follows, and within that culture the young ones start to catch it.

Make this a core value. Know that nothing becomes a value until you put time, effort, and money toward it. Invest in it. It will be the greatest venture you'll make in your growth and development. Spend the time necessary to develop a daily mentoring system with the Holy Spirit.

FINDING YOUR OASIS

I remember times when, as a young father with two babies in diapers, I couldn't simply sneak off to do devotions each morning, leaving the squalling children to their mother. Personal experience and past consequences cautioned me against it. I needed another option.

I would ask my wife for forty-five minutes alone, and I would go out to my car. The car actually became a refuge and an oasis for me. It was comfortable, I could play soft music on the stereo, and I could even run the air-conditioner now and then if it was hot outside. I decided I had to make the cultivation of my roots a high priority.

The bottom line: Find a way that works for you. Of course, if you're a spiritual giant like Susanna Wesley, you can just put an apron over your head (as she did) and forget the world during a few moments alone with the Lord!

If you haven't yet begun, now is the time to start. Try your hand at a journal entry.

1. Find today's Bible reading on the following schedule.
2. Read the passages and find one that speaks to your heart.
3, Follow the SOAP acrostic and begin. Find a sample journaling page at the end of this chapter and additional journaling pages beginning on page 221.

THROUGH-THE-BIBLE READING PLAN[5]

*Your personal reading schedule to take you through
the entire Bible within a year.*

JANUARY

1 ☐ Gen. 1, 2; Luke 1
2 ☐ Gen. 3–5; Luke 2
3 ☐ Gen. 6–8; Luke 3
4 ☐ Gen. 9–11; Luke 4
5 ☐ Gen. 12–14; Luke 5
6 ☐ Gen. 15–17; Luke 6
7 ☐ Gen. 18, 19; Ps. 3;
   Luke 7
8 ☐ Gen. 20–22; Luke 8
9 ☐ Gen. 23, 24; Luke 9
10 ☐ Gen. 25, 26; Ps. 6;
   Luke 10
11 ☐ Gen. 27, 28; Ps. 4;
   Luke 11
12 ☐ Gen. 29, 30; Luke 12
13 ☐ Gen. 31–33; Luke 13
14 ☐ Gen. 34–36; Luke 14
15 ☐ Gen. 37, 38; Ps. 7;
   Luke 15
16 ☐ Gen. 39–41; Luke 16
17 ☐ Gen. 42, 43; Ps. 5;
   Luke 17
18 ☐ Gen. 44–46; Luke 18
19 ☐ Gen. 47, 48; Ps. 10;
   Luke 19
20 ☐ Gen. 49, 50; Ps. 8;
   Luke 20
21 ☐ Ex. 1, 2; Ps. 88; Luke 21
22 ☐ Ex. 3–5; Luke 22
23 ☐ Ex. 6–8; Luke 23

24 ☐ Ex. 9–11; Luke 24
25 ☐ Ex. 12, 13; Ps. 21; Acts 1
26 ☐ Ex. 14–16; Acts 2
27 ☐ Ex. 17–20; Acts 3
28 ☐ Ex. 21, 22; Ps. 12; Acts 4
29 ☐ Ex. 23, 24; Ps. 14; Acts 5
30 ☐ Ex. 25–27; Acts 6
31 ☐ Ex. 28, 29; Acts 7

FEBRUARY

1 ☐ Ex. 30–32; Acts 8
2 ☐ Ex. 33, 34; Ps. 16; Acts 9
3 ☐ Ex. 35, 36; Acts 10
4 ☐ Ex. 37, 38; Ps. 19;
   Acts 11
5 ☐ Ex. 39, 40; Ps. 15;
   Acts 12
6 ☐ Lev. 1–3; Acts 13
7 ☐ Lev. 4–6; Acts 14
8 ☐ Lev. 7–9; Acts 15
9 ☐ Lev. 10–12; Acts 16
10 ☐ Lev. 13, 14; Acts 17
11 ☐ Lev. 15–17; Acts 18
12 ☐ Lev. 18, 19; Ps. 13;
   Acts 19
13 ☐ Lev. 20–22; Acts 20
14 ☐ Lev. 23, 24; Ps. 24;
   Acts 21
15 ☐ Lev. 25; Ps. 25–26;
   Acts 22
16 ☐ Lev. 26, 27; Acts 23

17 ☐ Num. 1, 2; Acts 24

18 ☐ Num. 3, 4; Acts 25

19 ☐ Num. 5, 6; Ps. 22; Acts 26

20 ☐ Num. 7; Ps. 23; Acts 27

21 ☐ Num. 8, 9; Acts 28

22 ☐ Num. 10, 11; Ps. 27; Mark 1

23 ☐ Num. 12, 13; Ps. 90; Mark 2

24 ☐ Num. 14–16; Mark 3

25 ☐ Num. 17, 18; Ps. 29; Mark 4

26 ☐ Num. 19, 20; Ps. 28; Mark 5

27 ☐ Num. 21–23; Mark 6, 7

28 ☐ Num. 24–27; 1 Cor. 13

MARCH

1 ☐ Num. 28, 29; Mark 8

2 ☐ Num. 30, 31; Mark 9

3 ☐ Num. 32, 33; Mark 10

4 ☐ Num. 34–36; Mark 11

5 ☐ Deut. 1, 2; Mark 12

6 ☐ Deut. 3, 4; Ps. 36; Mark 13

7 ☐ Deut. 5, 6; Ps. 43; Mark 14

8 ☐ Deut. 7–9; Mark 15

9 ☐ Deut. 10–12; Mark 16

10 ☐ Deut. 13–15; Gal. 1

11 ☐ Deut. 16–18; Ps. 38; Gal. 2

12 ☐ Deut. 19–21; Gal. 3

13 ☐ Deut. 22–24; Gal. 4

14 ☐ Deut. 25–27; Gal. 5

15 ☐ Deut. 28, 29; Gal. 6

16 ☐ Deut. 30, 31; Ps. 40; 1 Cor. 1

17 ☐ Deut. 32–34; 1 Cor. 2

18 ☐ Josh. 1, 2; Ps. 37; 1 Cor. 3

19 ☐ Josh. 3–6; 1 Cor. 4

20 ☐ Josh. 7, 8; Ps. 69; 1 Cor. 5

21 ☐ Josh. 9–11; 1 Cor. 6

22 ☐ Josh. 12–14; 1 Cor. 7

23 ☐ Josh. 15–17; 1 Cor. 8

24 ☐ Josh. 18–20; 1 Cor. 9

25 ☐ Josh. 21, 22; Ps. 47; 1 Cor. 10

26 ☐ Josh. 23, 24; Ps. 44; 1 Cor. 11

27 ☐ Judg. 1–3; 1 Cor. 12

28 ☐ Judg. 4, 5; Ps. 39, 41; 1 Cor. 13

29 ☐ Judg. 6, 7; Ps. 52; 1 Cor. 14

30 ☐ Judg. 8; Ps. 42; 1 Cor. 15

31 ☐ Judg. 9, 10; Ps. 49; 1 Cor. 16

APRIL

1 ☐ Judg. 11, 12; Ps. 50; 2 Cor. 1

2 ☐ Judg. 13–16; 2 Cor. 2

3 ☐ Judg. 17, 18; Ps. 89; 2 Cor. 3

4 ☐ Judg. 19–21; 2 Cor. 4

5 ☐ Ruth 1, 2; Ps. 53, 61; 2 Cor. 5

6 ☐ Ruth 3, 4; Ps. 64, 65; 2 Cor. 6

7 ☐ 1 Sam. 1, 2; Ps. 66; 2 Cor. 7

8 ☐ 1 Sam. 3–5; Ps. 77;
2 Cor. 8

9 ☐ 1 Sam. 6, 7; Ps. 72;
2 Cor. 9

10 ☐ 1 Sam. 8–10; 2 Cor. 10

11 ☐ 1 Sam. 11, 12; 1 Chr. 1;
2 Cor. 11

12 ☐ 1 Sam. 13; 1 Chr. 2, 3;
2 Cor. 12

13 ☐ 1 Sam. 14; 1 Chr. 4;
2 Cor. 13

14 ☐ 1 Sam. 15, 16; 1 Chr. 5;
Mt. 1

15 ☐ 1 Sam. 17; Ps. 9; Mt. 2

16 ☐ 1 Sam. 18; 1 Chr. 6;
Ps. 11; Mt. 3

17 ☐ 1 Sam. 19; 1 Chr. 7;
Ps. 59; Mt. 4

18 ☐ 1 Sam. 20, 21; Ps. 34;
Mt. 5

19 ☐ 1 Sam. 22; Ps. 17, 35;
Mt. 6

20 ☐ 1 Sam. 23; Ps. 31, 54;
Mt. 7

21 ☐ 1 Sam. 24; Ps. 57, 58;
1 Chr. 8; Mt. 8

22 ☐ 1 Sam. 25, 26; Ps. 63;
Mt. 9

23 ☐ 1 Sam. 27; Ps. 141;
1 Chr. 9; Mt. 10

24 ☐ 1 Sam. 28, 29; Ps. 109;
Mt. 11

25 ☐ 1 Sam. 30, 31; 1 Chr. 10;
Mt. 12

26 ☐ 2 Sam. 1; Ps. 140; Mt. 13

27 ☐ 2 Sam. 2; 1 Chr. 11;
Ps. 142; Mt. 14

28 ☐ 2 Sam. 3; 1 Chr. 12;
Mt. 15

29 ☐ 2 Sam. 4, 5; Ps. 139;
Mt. 16

30 ☐ 2 Sam. 6; 1 Chr. 13;
Ps. 68; Mt. 17

MAY

1 ☐ 1 Chr. 14, 15; Ps. 132;
Mt. 18

2 ☐ 1 Chr. 16; Ps. 106;
Mt. 19

3 ☐ 2 Sam. 7; 1 Chr. 17;
Ps. 2; Mt. 20

4 ☐ 2 Sam. 8, 9;
1 Chr. 18, 19; Mt. 21

5 ☐ 2 Sam. 10; 1 Chr. 20;
Ps. 20; Mt. 22

6 ☐ 2 Sam. 11, 12; Ps. 51;
Mt. 23

7 ☐ 2 Sam. 13, 14; Mt. 24

8 ☐ 2 Sam. 15, 16; Ps. 32;
Mt. 25

9 ☐ 2 Sam. 17; Ps. 71; Mt. 26

10 ☐ 2 Sam. 18; Ps. 56; Mt. 27

11 ☐ 2 Sam. 19, 20; Ps. 55;
Mt. 28

12 ☐ 2 Sam. 21–23; 1 Th. 1

13 ☐ 2 Sam. 24; 1 Chr. 21;
Ps. 30; 1 Th. 2

14 ☐ 1 Chr. 22–24; 1 Th. 3

15 ☐ 1 Chr. 25–27; 1 Th. 4

16 ☐ 1 Ki. 1; 1 Chr. 28; Ps. 91;
1 Th. 5

17 ☐ 1 Ki. 2; 1 Chr. 29; Ps. 95;
2 Th. 1

18 ☐ 1 Ki. 3; 2 Chr. 1; Ps. 78;
2 Th. 2

19 ☐ 1 Ki. 4, 5; 2 Chr. 2;
Ps. 101; 2 Th. 3

20 ☐ 1 Ki. 6; 2 Chr. 3; Ps. 97;
Rom. 1

21 ☐ 1 Ki. 7; 2 Chr. 4; Ps. 98;
Rom. 2

22 ☐ 1 Ki. 8; 2 Chr. 5; Ps. 99;
Rom. 3

23 ☐ 2 Chr. 6, 7; Ps. 135;
Rom. 4

24 ☐ 1 Ki. 9; 2 Chr. 8; Ps. 136;
Rom. 5

25 ☐ 1 Ki. 10, 11; 2 Chr. 9;
Rom. 6

26 ☐ Prov. 1–3; Rom. 7

27 ☐ Prov. 4–6; Rom. 8

28 ☐ Prov. 7–9; Rom. 9

29 ☐ Prov. 10–12; Rom. 10

30 ☐ Prov. 13–15; Rom. 11

31 ☐ Prov. 16–18; Rom. 12

JUNE

1 ☐ Prov. 19–21; Rom. 13

2 ☐ Prov. 22–24; Rom. 14

3 ☐ Prov. 25–27; Rom. 15

4 ☐ Prov. 28–29; Ps. 60;
Rom. 16

5 ☐ Prov. 30, 31; Ps. 33;
Eph. 1

6 ☐ Ecc. 1–3; Ps. 45; Eph. 2

7 ☐ Ecc. 4–6; Ps. 18; Eph. 3

8 ☐ Ecc. 7–9; Eph. 4

9 ☐ Ecc. 10–12; Ps. 94; Eph. 5

10 ☐ Song 1–4; Eph. 6

11 ☐ Song 5–8; Phil. 1

12 ☐ 1 Ki. 12; 2 Chr. 10, 11;
Phil. 2

13 ☐ 1 Ki. 13, 14; 2 Chr. 12;
Phil. 3

14 ☐ 1 Ki. 15; 2 Chr. 13, 14;
Phil. 4

15 ☐ 1 Ki. 16; 2 Chr. 15;16;
Col. 1

16 ☐ 1 Ki. 17–19; Col. 2

17 ☐ 1 Ki. 20, 21; 2 Chr. 17;
Col. 3

18 ☐ 1 Ki. 22; 2 Chr. 18, 19;
Col. 4

19 ☐ 2 Ki. 1–3; Ps. 82;
1 Tim. 1

20 ☐ 2 Ki. 4, 5; Ps. 83;
1 Tim. 2

21 ☐ 2 Ki. 6, 7; 2 Chr. 20;
1 Tim. 3

22 ☐ 2 Ki. 8, 9; 2 Chr. 21;
1 Tim. 4

23 ☐ 2 Ki. 10; 2 Chr. 22, 23;
1 Tim. 5

24 ☐ 2 Ki. 11, 12; 2 Chr. 24;
1 Tim. 6

25 ☐ Joel 1–3; 2 Tim. 1

26 ☐ Jon. 1–4; 2 Tim. 2

27 ☐ 2 Ki. 13, 14; 2 Chr. 25;
2 Tim. 3

28 ☐ Amos 1–3; Ps. 80;
2 Tim. 4

29 ☐ Amos 4–6; Ps. 86, 87;
Tit. 1

30 ☐ Amos 7–9; Ps. 104; Tit. 2

JULY

1 ☐ Is. 1–3; Tit. 3

2 ☐ Is. 4, 5; Ps. 115, 116;
Jude

3 ☐ Is. 6, 7; 2 Chr. 26, 27;
Philem.

4 ☐ 2 Ki. 15, 16; Hos. 1; Heb. 1

5 ☐ Hos. 2–5; Heb. 2

6 ☐ Hos. 6–9; Heb. 3

7 ☐ Hos. 10–12; Ps. 73; Heb. 4

8 ☐ Hos. 13, 14; Ps.100, 102; Heb. 5

9 ☐ Mic. 1–4; Heb. 6

10 ☐ Mic. 5–7; Heb. 7

11 ☐ Is. 8–10; Heb. 8

12 ☐ Is. 11–14; Heb. 9

13 ☐ Is. 15–18; Heb. 10

14 ☐ Is. 19–21; Heb. 11

15 ☐ Is. 22–24; Heb. 12

16 ☐ Is. 25–28; Heb. 13

17 ☐ Is. 29–31; Jas. 1

18 ☐ Is. 32–35; Jas. 2

19 ☐ 2 Ki. 17; 2 Chr. 28; Ps. 46; Jas. 3

20 ☐ 2 Chr. 29–31; Jas. 4

21 ☐ 2 Ki. 18, 19; 2 Chr. 32; Jas. 5

22 ☐ Is. 36, 37; Ps. 76; 1 Pet. 1

23 ☐ 2 Ki. 20; Is. 38, 39; Ps. 75; 1 Pet. 2

24 ☐ Is. 40–42; 1 Pet. 3

25 ☐ Is. 43–45; 1 Pet. 4

26 ☐ Is. 46–49; 1 Pet. 5

27 ☐ Is. 50–52; Ps. 92; 2 Pet. 1

28 ☐ Is. 53–56; 2 Pet. 2

29 ☐ Is. 57–59; Ps. 103; 2 Pet. 3

30 ☐ Is. 60–62; Jn. 1

31 ☐ Is. 63, 64; Ps. 107; Jn. 2

AUGUST

1 ☐ Is. 65, 66; Ps. 62; Jn. 3

2 ☐ 2 Ki. 21; 2 Chr. 33, Jn. 4

3 ☐ Nah. 1–3; Jn. 5

4 ☐ 2 Ki. 22; 2 Chr. 34; Jn. 6

5 ☐ 2 Ki. 23; 2 Chr. 35; Jn. 7

6 ☐ Hab. 1–3; Jn. 8

7 ☐ Zeph. 1–3; Jn. 9

8 ☐ Jer. 1, 2; Jn. 10

9 ☐ Jer. 3, 4; Jn. 11

10 ☐ Jer. 5, 6; Jn. 12

11 ☐ Jer. 7–9; Jn. 13

12 ☐ Jer. 10–12; Jn. 14

13 ☐ Jer. 13–15; Jn. 15

14 ☐ Jer. 16, 17; Ps. 96; Jn. 16

15 ☐ Jer. 18–20; Ps. 93; Jn. 17

16 ☐ 2 Ki. 24; Jer. 22; Ps. 112; Jn. 18

17 ☐ Jer. 23, 25; Jn. 19

18 ☐ Jer. 26, 35, 36; Jn. 20

19 ☐ Jer. 45–47; Ps. 105; Jn. 21

20 ☐ Jer. 48, 49; Ps. 67; 1 Jn. 1

21 ☐ Jer. 21, 24, 27; Ps. 118; 1 Jn. 2

22 ☐ Jer. 28–30; 1 Jn. 3

23 ☐ Jer. 31, 32; 1 Jn. 4

24 ☐ Jer. 33, 34; Ps. 74; 1 Jn. 5

25 ☐ Jer. 37–39; Ps. 79; 2 Jn.

26 ☐ Jer. 50, 51; 3 Jn.

27 ☐ Jer. 52; Rev. 1; Ps. 143, 144

28 ☐ Ezek. 1–3; Rev. 2

29 ☐ Ezek. 4–7; Rev. 3

30 ☐ Ezek. 8–11; Rev. 4

31 ☐ Ezek. 12–14; Rev. 5

SEPTEMBER

1 ☐ Ezek. 15, 16; Ps. 70; Rev. 6

2 ☐ Ezek. 17–19; Rev. 7

3 ☐ Ezek. 20, 21; Ps. 111;
Rev. 8

4 ☐ Ezek. 22–24; Rev. 9

5 ☐ Ezek. 25–28; Rev. 10

6 ☐ Ezek. 29–32; Rev. 11

7 ☐ 2 Ki. 25; 2 Chr. 36;
Jer. 40, 41; Rev. 12

8 ☐ Jer. 42–44; Ps. 48; Rev. 13

9 ☐ Lam. 1, 2; Obad.; Rev. 14

10 ☐ Lam. 3–5; Rev. 15

11 ☐ Dan. 1, 2; Rev. 16

12 ☐ Dan. 3, 4; Ps. 81; Rev. 17

13 ☐ Ezek. 33–35; Rev. 18

14 ☐ Ezek. 36, 37; Ps. 110;
Rev. 19

15 ☐ Ezek. 38, 39; Ps. 145;
Rev. 20

16 ☐ Ezek. 40, 41; Ps. 128;
Rev. 21

17 ☐ Ezek. 42–44; Rev. 22

18 ☐ Ezek. 45, 46; Lk. 1

19 ☐ Ezek. 47, 48; Lk. 2

20 ☐ Dan. 5, 6; Ps. 130; Lk. 3

21 ☐ Dan. 7, 8; Ps. 137; Lk. 4

22 ☐ Dan. 9, 10; Ps. 123; Lk. 5

23 ☐ Dan. 11, 12; Lk. 6

24 ☐ Ezra 1; Ps. 84, 85; Lk. 7

25 ☐ Ezra 2, 3; Lk. 8

26 ☐ Ezra 4; Ps. 113, 127;
Lk. 9

27 ☐ Hag. 1, 2; Ps. 129; Lk. 10

28 ☐ Zech. 1–3; Lk. 11

29 ☐ Zech. 4–6; Lk. 12

30 ☐ Zech. 7–9; Lk. 13

OCTOBER

1 ☐ Zech. 10–12; Ps. 126;
Lk. 14

2 ☐ Zech. 13–14; Ps. 147;
Lk. 15

3 ☐ Ezra 5, 6; Ps. 138; Lk. 16

4 ☐ Est. 1, 2; Ps. 150; Lk. 17

5 ☐ Est. 3–8; Lk. 18

6 ☐ Est. 9–10; Lk. 19

7 ☐ Ezra 7, 8; Lk. 20

8 ☐ Ezra 9, 10; Ps. 131;
Lk. 21

9 ☐ Neh. 1, 2; Ps. 133, 134;
Lk. 22

10 ☐ Neh. 3, 4; Lk. 23

11 ☐ Neh. 5, 6; Ps. 146; Lk. 24

12 ☐ Neh. 7, 8; Acts 1

13 ☐ Neh. 9, 10; Acts 2

14 ☐ Neh. 11, 12; Ps. 1; Acts 3

15 ☐ Neh. 13; Mal. 1, 2; Acts 4

16 ☐ Mal. 3, 4; Ps. 148; Acts 5

17 ☐ Job 1, 2; Acts 6, 7

18 ☐ Job 3, 4; Acts 8, 9

19 ☐ Job 5; Ps. 108;
Acts 10, 11

20 ☐ Job 6–8; Acts 12

21 ☐ Job 9, 10; Acts 13, 14

22 ☐ Job 11, 12; Acts 15, 16

23 ☐ Job 13, 14; Acts 17, 18

24 ☐ Job 15; Acts 19, 20

25 ☐ Job 16; Acts 21–23

26 ☐ Job 17; Acts 24–26

27 ☐ Job 18; Ps. 114;
Acts 27, 28

28 ☐ Job 19; Mk. 1, 2

29 ☐ Job 20; Mk. 3, 4

30 ☐ Job 21; Mk. 5, 6

31 ☐ Job 22; Mk. 7, 8

NOVEMBER

1 ☐ Ps. 121; Mk. 9, 10

2 ☐ Job 23, 24; Mk. 11, 12

3 ☐ Job 25; Mk. 13, 14
4 ☐ Job 26, 27; Mk. 15, 16
5 ☐ Job 28, 29; Gal. 1, 2
6 ☐ Job 30; Ps. 120; Gal. 3, 4
7 ☐ Job 31, 32; Gal. 5, 6
8 ☐ Job 33; 1 Cor. 1–3
9 ☐ Job 34; 1 Cor. 4–6
10 ☐ Job 35, 36; 1 Cor. 7–8
11 ☐ Ps. 122; 1 Cor. 9–11
12 ☐ Job 37, 38; 1 Cor. 12
13 ☐ Job 39, 40; 1 Cor. 13, 14
14 ☐ Ps. 149; 1 Cor. 15, 16
15 ☐ Job 41, 42; 2 Cor. 1, 2
16 ☐ 2 Cor. 3–6
17 ☐ 2 Cor. 7–10
18 ☐ Ps. 124; 2 Cor. 11–13
19 ☐ Mt. 1–4
20 ☐ Mt. 5–7
21 ☐ Mt. 8–10
22 ☐ Mt. 11–13
23 ☐ Mt. 14–16
24 ☐ Mt. 17–19
25 ☐ Mt. 20–22
26 ☐ Mt. 23–25
27 ☐ Ps. 125; Mt. 26, 27
28 ☐ Mt. 28; 1 Th. 1–3
29 ☐ 1 Th. 4, 5; 2 Th. 1–3
30 ☐ Rom. 1–4

9 ☐ 1 Tim. 5, 6; Tit. 1–3
10 ☐ 2 Tim. 1–4
11 ☐ Philem.; Heb. 1–4
12 ☐ Heb. 5–8
13 ☐ Heb. 9–11
14 ☐ Heb. 12, 13; Jude
15 ☐ Jas. 1–5
16 ☐ 1 Pet. 1–5
17 ☐ 2 Pet. 1–3; Jn. 1
18 ☐ Jn. 2–4
19 ☐ Jn. 5, 6
20 ☐ Jn. 7, 8
21 ☐ Jn. 9–11
22 ☐ Jn. 12–14
23 ☐ Jn. 15–18
24 ☐ Jn. 19–21
25 ☐ 1 Jn. 1–5
26 ☐ Ps. 117, 119:81–176;
       2 Jn.; 3 Jn.
27 ☐ Rev. 1–4
28 ☐ Rev. 5–9
29 ☐ Rev. 10–14
30 ☐ Rev. 15–18
31 ☐ Rev. 19–22

DECEMBER

1 ☐ Rom. 5–8
2 ☐ Rom. 9–12
3 ☐ Rom. 13–16
4 ☐ Eph. 1–4
5 ☐ Eph. 5, 6; Ps. 119:1–80
6 ☐ Phil. 1–4
7 ☐ Col. 1–4
8 ☐ 1 Tim. 1–4

Title:

// SCRIPTURE

// OBSERVATION

// APPLICATION

// PRAYER

11

Delighting
in God's Word

Your words were found and I ate them,
and Your words became for me a joy
and the delight of my heart.[1]

A few years ago I made a teaching trip to China. Twenty leaders of the house church movement from a nearby province came together for leadership training. I was told to be ready to stand up at 8:00 A.M. and teach until 6:00 P.M.—thankfully, with a short break for lunch. We'd repeat the regimen for three days. It was fatiguing, demanding, and one of the most moving experiences of my life.

They endured a thirteen-hour train ride. Meeting at a predetermined location, they arrived alone or in twos so as not to arouse suspicion. Gathering together in a small, stifling room, they sat cross-legged on a wooden floor. Most were humble farmers. Every face was weathered with deep lines that held stories of profound trial and supernatural perseverance.

Sometimes when you speak to a large group, you hope that 20 to 25 percent (on a good day) will actually absorb what you're saying. In this group, it was every person in the room!

The huge smiles on all the faces brightened their simple clothing. They were hungry and eager to hear from the narrators of the Bible. Their eagerness would extract the best from me. They were soaking in everything as though they would never be in such a meeting again . . . which was certainly a possibility. When they raised their hands in worship, I saw at least one man with scars from the shackles that had been his companions in prison.

Shortly after we began, to get us more acquainted, I asked them to say a little about who they were. One reported with joy that he'd just been released from serving his fifth three-year term in jail.

His crime? Faith in an unseen Messiah.

"How many others of you have spent time in prison for your faith?" I asked.

Eighteen of the twenty raised their hands.

"If government authorities discovered this non-registered religious meeting, what would happen?"

They answered, "Each would be given a three-year prison sentence, and we would be deported within twenty-four hours."

"Aren't you afraid?" I inquired.

"No," they said with a quiet confidence. "We are not afraid. And if you will teach us for another day, we will stay."

I commended them for their faith, all the while wondering why *they* weren't teaching *me* instead of the other way around.

Since I knew that each of these veteran saints oversaw large numbers of house churches, I continued my let's-get-acquainted session by asking, "How many people do you oversee in all the house churches, combined?"

After a moment of quiet calculation, one spoke up.

"Twenty-two million."

I couldn't believe I'd heard what I just heard. "Twenty—

twenty-two *million?*" I stammered.

"Yes," he nodded. "Twenty-two million."

After a few moments, I caught my breath and launched into teaching. We'd brought sixteen Bibles to pass out, leaving a few of the leaders to share with one another. I had them turn to Second Peter, chapter 1. As we were about to read it out loud, one elderly woman handed her Bible to another leader. I thought that was a bit strange, since Bibles were so scarce, but I didn't call attention to the matter.

After we began to read, I understood why she had willingly given up her Bible.

She quoted the whole chapter *from memory!*

During a short break, I asked her how she memorized so much Scripture. "I have much more memorized," she replied through one of our interpreters.

"But how did you memorize so much," I asked, "when there are so few Bibles available?"

"In prison," she said.

Pushing back, I went on. "But if you had a Bible, wouldn't they confiscate it right away?"

"Yes," she answered. "So people brought me Scriptures written on pieces of paper."

"And what if the guards found you with those?" I pressed. "Wouldn't they take away those as well?"

"Yes. That is why I memorized the Scriptures as quickly as I could. You see, they can take away the paper, but *they cannot take away what I have already hidden in my heart.*"

By the end of two days, I had fallen in love with this part of God's family. Realizing my own inadequacy to help them in their daunting task of reaching China, I asked them in our final session together: "How can I pray for you?"

"Pray that we become like you," was their immediate request.

One of my newfound friends continued: "We do not have

freedom of religion. We have only a few registered churches, and when the pews are filled, they turn the others away. But in your country, you can gather whenever you like." He concluded by saying, again, "Pray that we can one day be like you!"

I shook my head sadly. "I can't do that. I can't pray for you in that way."

"But why?" they asked incredulously.

With a sigh, I explained. "You came here after riding thirteen hours on a train. In America, if church is more than thirty minutes away, people won't go. It's too far.

"You have been sitting on a wooden floor without air-conditioning for three days. Where I come from, if people can't sit on cushioned chairs and be in the comfort of air-conditioning, they'll find better things to do.

"You don't have adequate Bibles, so you memorize Scriptures from pieces of paper. In American Christian homes, we have multiple Bibles per family, but we don't always read them.

"No," I said. "I will not pray that you become like us. But I will pray . . . that we become *like you!*"

A BOOK LIKE NO OTHER

Why did these Chinese leaders take such a huge risk, gathering as a group to hear God's Word? Why did they value the Bible's wisdom so much that they placed their very lives in jeopardy in order to listen to the Lord's voice?

Because they know by experience the Word's power and truth. They know that no weapon but the sword of the Spirit delivers the might to tear down spiritual fortresses and conquer enemy sanctuaries. They believe the Lord when He asks, "Is not my word like fire . . . and like a hammer that breaks a rock in pieces?"[2] And they believe the apostle when he declares, "Though we live in the world, we do not wage war as the world does. The weapons we fight with are not the weapons of the world. On the contrary, they have divine power to demolish strongholds. We demolish arguments and every pretension that sets itself up against the knowledge of God, and we take captive every thought to make it obedient to Christ."[3]

These leaders understand that the Bible is like no other book in all the world. They recognize its matchless authority as well as its supernatural ability, through the Spirit, to speak truth directly into our hearts so that we are enabled, literally, to become more like Christ.

We sometimes call the Bible the "Book of books." That simply means it stands out above all other writings that have ever been or ever will be published.

The management of various hotels might place other so-called holy books in nightstand drawers next to the beds. Those can't touch the Bible.

It doesn't matter if they're bound in leather, touched up with gilt pages and silk ribbons, and printed on the finest India paper. They're only books, and that's all they'll ever be. One day they will burn, and when they do they won't stir even the vaguest memory in eternity.

No other book compares with the Word of God. Let me show you how He has set this Book apart from all others.

(1) THE BIBLE IS THE ONLY BOOK GOD EVER PROMISED TO INSPIRE

It's good to read classics like *Mere Christianity, My Utmost for His Highest,* or *Streams in the Desert,* but not one of these is inspired in the same way the Bible is. God promised to inspire only one book, and that is His own Word.

> Know this first of all, that no prophecy of Scripture is a matter of one's own interpretation, for no prophecy was ever made by an act of human will, but men moved by the Holy Spirit spoke from God.[4]

All Scripture is inspired by God and profitable for teaching, for reproof, for correction, for training in righteousness; so that the man of God may be adequate, equipped for every good work.[5]

If you want to hear the words that God himself breathed into existence, you must go to His Word. Other volumes may give you helpful insights, engaging stories, unique perspectives, and memorable concepts, but the Bible is the one book that will give you God's mind on every page and in every paragraph, sentence, and word.

(2) THE BIBLE IS THE ONLY BOOK WHERE ALL THE DIVINE MENTORS ARE PRESENT

There are many phenomenal literary mentors from whom you can learn—Milton, Bunyan, Shakespeare, Dostoevsky among them. There are multitudes of brilliant and insightful historical mentors, such as Winston Churchill, Abraham Lincoln, Teresa of Avila, and Florence Nightingale. There are also contemporary mentors: my friend Duane was such a mentor to me years ago when I worked with Youth for Christ. We'd meet every week to discuss issues of life and ministry, and I'll never forget how he invested himself in me.

But there's only one Book in which you can meet with *all* the mentors specially selected by God to teach the saints. Only the Bible's men and women are His designated divine mentors. He has put His imprimatur on them alone. Jesus recognized this and so treated these men and women as His own divine mentors when He memorized their words, quoted from their books, and preached from their example.

Even when engulfed in a fire of agony, hanging on wooden beams by nails driven through His hands and feet—even then He quoted the words of David: *"My God, my God, why have You forsaken me?"*[6]

So if the Lord puts His full weight behind these mentors—

and the solitary book where they all live—don't you think we should as well?

(3) GOD PROMISES SPECIFICALLY TO BLESS THE READERS OF THE BIBLE

God never says, "If you read C. S. Lewis, I will bless you." He might do that, but He makes no such promise. He never says, "If you'll pick up the most recent book from your favorite author, I'll bless you." He never promises to bless the readers of *any* book except the one He authored. Not Augustine, not Charles Spurgeon, not Dwight L. Moody, not Amy Carmichael, and not Billy Graham. All these are wonderful and worthy of our reading, but only one will be called "The Word of God."

Listen to what He offers in the Bible's last book, a unique promise uttered nowhere else. When God had completed His Book, He spoke the following words through His servant John:

> John . . . testifies to everything he saw—that is, the word of God and the testimony of Jesus Christ. Blessed is the one who reads the words of this prophecy, and blessed are those who hear it and take to heart what is written in it, because the time is near.[7]

If you want a sure blessing from God, the surest way to get it is to read the only book He's inspired. You have His promise!

(4) THE BIBLE IS THE ONLY BOOK THAT WILL LIVE FOREVER

> The grass withers, the flower fades, but the word of our God stands forever.[8]

We often talk about "immortal" books that will last through the ages, but the fact is, most of these are forgotten as soon as some new "immortal" book comes along. The bestsellers of yesterday are rarely the bestsellers of today.

With one major exception, of course.

The Bible remains the bestselling book on the planet, a position it has occupied from the time books first were printed. Skeptics, dictators, antagonists, and many others have tried to stamp out the Word and remove it from existence.

But it's a funny thing. The Bible's opponents keep dying, while the Bible lives on and on. The French Enlightenment hero Voltaire once claimed that through his efforts and those of likeminded rationalists, the Bible would disappear from the planet within a generation. A generation later, his house was being used to print Bibles.

Here's what God says about the longevity of His book:

- •• "Your word, O Lord, is eternal; it stands firm in the heavens."[9]
- •• "Truly I say to you, until heaven and earth pass away, not the smallest letter or stroke shall pass from the Law until all is accomplished."[10]

Someday in heaven, whether it's a week or a millennium from now, you might be lounging in your celestial mansion, listening to an angelic choir while you meditate on John 3:16.

You really might!

Because God's Word will still be there, living and active, offering you His inexhaustible wisdom.

INSPIRED: TRUSTWORTHY AND ACCURATE

The Bible's infallibility can be found in its 100 percent accuracy in predicting the future. These are called *prophecies*. The Old Testament, written between about 1450 BC and 430 BC, predicted many of the future events that were later recorded. These occurrences took place exactly as they were prophesied. There is no other "sacred writing" with such an accurate record.

Of the many recorded prophecies, the most compelling are the predictions about an "anointed one" ("Messiah" in Hebrew) who would redeem His people. A miraculous event occurred around 4 BC. A child named Jesus was born to a virgin named Mary; Luke's gospel records His story in detail. Then, beginning at age thirty, Jesus increasingly began to fulfill more and more of these prophecies written about the Jewish Messiah, whose genealogy would record Him as a descendent of David.

The fulfillment of these prophecies was spectacular. Jesus made the lame to walk, healed the lepers, gave sight to the blind, granted hearing to the deaf, and raised people from the dead. These and many other miracles took place in front of thousands of witnesses for three and a half years.

Around AD 30, Jesus was crucified as a common thief on a cross. He died, and on the third day He rose from the dead (these events fulfilling three more prophecies). Over five hundred witnesses then saw Him.

The prophecies were written down hundreds of years before they were fulfilled; there is no doubt that the Bible's writers were supernaturally inspired by God.

Packaging and Handling

That the Word is "immortal" doesn't mean it cannot be misinterpreted. The Pharisees seemed to excel at this. In one conversation between the Messiah and His naysayers, "Jesus said to them, 'Is this not the reason you are mistaken, that you do not understand the Scriptures or the power of God?' "[11]

It was in the early 1500s—only five hundred years ago—that the clergy actually chained the Bible to the pulpit so no one could take it home. The Great Bible, authorized by King Henry VIII, was to be read aloud in the Church of England. Obviously the trained clergy knew best how to interpret the Scriptures; therefore, they alone should read it and subsequently enlighten the commoners as to its meaning.

It would be during this season of history that Girolamo

Savonarola would preach against clerical corruption until he was executed.

A young William Tyndale was horrified that he was allowed to study theology but not the Scriptures. Tyndale was convinced that the way to God was through God's Word and that the Scriptures should be available to all. In 1525, he finished translating the Bible into the common language of the people.

John Calvin would also appear on the scene, denouncing the dishonesty of church leaders and helping to ignite the Reformation.

Precursors to the Reformation were men like John Wycliffe and Martin Luther, who rallied in dispute of the misreading and misapplication of Scripture . . . not by commoners, but by the clergy.

Whenever a revival began or a reformation occurred, its epicenter was among common people who were ignited by the Word of God. It began with a returning to their roots and a reclaiming of their inheritance.

Discerning the signs of the times, we are in time's concluding days. I do not know which part of the last chapter we are in, but we are in the final chapter. And we will be faced with a choice: a falling away or a pressing in. It will be a defining moment for the church.

Paul forecasted this:

> The Spirit explicitly says that in later times some will fall away from the faith, paying attention to deceitful spirits and doctrines of demons.[12]

Some people's attention will be held captive by false leadings, and they will be gullible to tempting but deceptive words. Only by knowing the Shepherd's voice will God's people be kept from being tossed to and fro. It is by knowing the Scriptures that we will be able to discern truth from error, light from darkness.

Slipped Treasures

// SCRIPTURE

*Many are the afflictions of the righteous, but the Lord
delivers him out of them all. (Psalm 34:19)*

// OBSERVATION

It would have been much better, in my estimation anyway, if that verse read:
"The righteous will have zero afflictions; they will each be given a 'Smooth Riding'
guarantee." But it doesn't.

David wrote this psalm, and his life was not a leisure ride—it was replete with
challenges and scored by struggles. Yet his life emerges as the quintessence of
Israel's best.

// APPLICATION

It says, *"Many are the afflictions of the righteous."* Does that mean the reward
of trying our best will be pain? Why would God want us to experience afflictions in
the first place?

When I reflect back on my life, I realize the times I grew the most came
wrapped in "struggle paper." You see, the greatest gems are not found on moun-
taintops. They tumble to the valley floor.

They are not always new treasures, but maybe *slipped treasures* that have long
been missing in my life.

An appreciation misplaced. A love that's been absent. A commitment that's
been lost. A vision that's strayed. A heart mislaid.

And when they're restored, I am delivered from the consequences of living
without them.

Afflictions are not fun. For many years I preferred fun to growth. Now I must
make a choice: Do I need more fun, or do I need more growth?

I've decided I need to grow . . . but with just a little fun thrown in.

// PRAYER

Father, I'm always stirred by Your Word and how it speaks more clearly to
me than this morning's newspaper. I will renew the values of my heart today.
Thank You for giving me a future and a hope.

AGAIN: CORRECTING BACK TO THE SOURCE

The best interpretation of the Bible is the Bible itself—not another book, not a denomination's teaching. Always correct everything you read back to the actions and the spirit of Jesus Christ. Go all the way back to Him. Not to an evangelist, not to another book you read, and not to something you saw on TV.

Always correct back to the Source.

When I was in junior high, my dad decided to build a fence. He wanted the boards spaced a certain distance apart to let air through, so the fence wouldn't suffer water damage. For this, he needed spacers between the boards.

"Wayne," he said, "I need you to cut two-inch spacers off of these two-by-fours. Here's how you do it. You cut it, and then you take this two-inch piece as your mark. Use it to mark all the other boards. Got it?"

"Got it, Dad. I can do that." (How hard could it be?)

"Okay. I'll need a couple hundred of them, so you'd better get busy."

I took a two-by-four, marked it off just as he'd shown me, then cut it. I used the cut piece to mark the next one, then I threw the marker piece aside. I cut the next measurement, used it to measure the next, and then threw it into the pile . . . just like my dad had explained.

Well, not *exactly* as my dad had explained. But I had a system going, and I really had the groove. I was certain he would be pleased at all the work I was getting done.

As the process continued, it never occurred to me that I was adding the width of the pencil's lead to each additional spacer. Now, that may not seem like much, but after two hundred repetitions, the width adds up quickly.

Can you see where this is going?

Around lunchtime we stopped to eat, and my dad finally had a chance to look at his fence. To that point he'd kept himself busy nailing boards and spacers. But now he stepped back to survey what we had created.

A puzzled expression came over his face. "Man," he exclaimed, "this fence is looking ugly!" He picked up one of the last spacers I'd made, measured it, and discovered it was nearly three inches instead of the prescribed two inches. He was not a happy camper.

"What were you *doing*?" he demanded.

When I demonstrated my system, he came unglued. "You *always* use the original piece to mark the next!"

A lot of Christians make the same kind of mistake. They get off track somehow and then try to correct back to their favorite contemporary author, conference speaker, or denominational stand. While those may be fine, God didn't use any of them to write Scripture.

You always correct back to the Source.

THE Source.

You just can't afford not to.

SPOKESPERSONS FOR GOD

As we become people shaped daily by God's Word, we can become spokespersons He can use. Hear His intriguing word to Jeremiah:

> If you extract the precious from the worthless, you will become My spokesman.[13]

When we learn how to extract the precious from the worthless, we can earn an invitation to speak for God. Actually speak for God. An incredible thought!

God isn't looking for someone loaded down with churchy buzzwords and Christian clichés. He doesn't need someone with a Master's degree in marketing or a PhD in public relations. Nor does He need public speakers who manipulate people with guilt or shame into praying more, giving more, doing more.

God is calling for a spokesperson—*a man or woman who will deliver His very heart*. He's looking for someone who will speak in such a way that a light will turn on. He is searching for those who will know His heart and His passion for the lost.

BEGGING FOR A CHANGE

A friend of mine is a pastor in Japan. One day he told me how he received the Lord. In college he had a Christian roommate. My friend was a Buddhist who wanted nothing to do with Jesus, yet this roommate would pray for him every day. Finally, on the day of graduation, they were about to depart and go their separate ways.

"Please, John," the young Christian said with tears in his eyes. "I've taken you to Bible studies. I've taken you to church. Please give your heart to the Lord."

"No," John replied. "*No.*"

"Please."

"No," he repeated.

His roommate then got on his knees and said, "I beg you, please."

"No," John said again, insistently.

A short while later, however, when John pondered the encounter, he thought, *You know, I've never had anyone beg me to give my heart to Christ. He must love me a whole lot.*

And that was what started the ball rolling. John not only received Christ, but eventually he studied for the ministry, and now he pastors a thriving church in Okinawa. Through a spokesman who knew how to extract the precious from the worthless, God's heart came to John, not in wrath or in judgment but in compassion and love.

God is still looking for spokesmen and spokeswomen with

that kind of heart, to deliver His word to a world caught in the darkness between heaven and earth.

REFLECTING OUR SURROUNDINGS—FOR BETTER OR WORSE

Wouldn't it be an honor and a privilege to be a spokesperson for God?

"So what does it take?" you ask.

A good place to start is by staying near to God's heart. When you stay near to the Lord's heart, you become more like Him. You begin to understand what He's saying, how He's saying things, the words He uses—even His inflections—and you start doing and saying the same things.

That's what happened with Peter and John, as described in the book of Acts. They'd hung (and hung, and hung) around Jesus, and others noticed something different about them:

> As they observed the confidence of Peter and John and understood that they were uneducated and untrained men, they were amazed, and began to recognize them as having been with Jesus.[14]

You can't hang out with somebody for long without picking up a little of him or her—without his or her character rubbing off on you. Jesus said, "Everyone who is fully trained will be like his teacher."[15]

That's why Paul also said to be careful which friends you choose, because "bad company corrupts good morals."[16] You will become like those with whom you spend significant time.

Some years ago a *Baywatch* special starring David Hasselhoff was being filmed in Hawaii. Alex Daniels, who was attending our church at the time, acted as his stuntman double. I was invited to go on the set for a closer look.

Outside Hasselhoff's trailer was a set of dumbbells so he

could buff up before he went out to the beach. There an attractive group of models was already gathering. It was thrilling, just hobnobbing with all the celebrities; I thought, *Hey, I could get used to this!*

Sometime during the second or third day I found myself morphing. I walked a little taller, and a suave demeanor began to descend on me . . . sort of an Elvis Presley look and feel. My voice even took on a deeper resonance.

Then I remember passing by a mirror near one of the actor's trailers. I saw my reflection and thought, *Yikes. What have I become? I'd better get back home to reality!*

It wasn't a pretty sight.

Of course, it works the other way around too. Some time ago I used to hang around with a dear elderly man named Noel Campbell. He had helped me pioneer a church in Hilo. He was a prince of a man, and he would always finish his conversations with "I sure love you."

And it wasn't just talk. He was as genuine as the Hawaiian sunshine. I could always count on him for an encouraging word. Once in a blue moon, I'd preach a home-run sermon, and after church I'd be tempted to take a couple of extra laps around the parking lot waving to parishioners. But more often than not it would resemble a flop. When I'd preached a horrible sermon and I'd sneak out the back door, he would find me and say, "I sure love you."

"I'm so glad one person does," I remember saying.

Noel finally retired and returned to Spokane, Washington. And do you know what happened? Soon I found myself finishing many of my conversations with "I sure love you."

And I actually meant it.

It's a good thing to pick up positive habits from those you spend time with. Even so, no matter how great your friends are, there's none better to hang around with than the mentors of the Scriptures.

JUST ONE PERSON, ONE LIGHT

As we become consistent in our daily devotions, we begin to understand what it means to be a spokesperson for God. Our words become more like His words. They build up, give life, and are always motivated by love. Do you know what happens when your words start to carry that quality? *The Lord's words start to define you as His disciple.*

> The Lord God has given Me the tongue of disciples, that I may know how to sustain the weary one with a word.[17]

We don't need people who are merely slick in presentation or eloquent in oratory. Hurting people don't need another churchy cliché. They don't need religious words. *They need someone—one person—who will speak for God.*

A husband and wife are tired of struggling. *They need someone who will speak for God.*

A troubled co-worker is at a dead end. *He needs someone who will speak for God.*

When a loved one is diagnosed with cancer, or when a minister is discouraged, or when a saint is caught in sin, they don't need a religious assassinator. They need a genuine ambassador.

Be one, my friend, and delight the heart of God.

The story is told of a World War II expedition with six planes that launched from a Navy carrier. They dropped their payloads, and under the shroud of night began to make their way back.

Radioing to the ship, they called for increased lighting on the rough seas so they could find their approach on the steeping deck. The call came back that they were to maintain a complete blackout due to enemy planes in surveillance of Allied ships.

The pilots called back an SOS pleading for lights because without them they'd be unable to find the ship in the pitch-dark ocean. The radio operator refused their pleas.

"Then just one light," the lead pilot begged. "Just one on the bow, and we will take our chances!"

"We're only following our orders," the operator radioed back. "I'm sorry. Really sorry," and the tower's communication lines went dead.

All six planes were lost.

Millions are stranded, desperately searching for a way to God. They've experimented with counterfeits, settled for the world, and still are empty and in need. They are looking for *just one light* that would lead them home.

GOING DEEPER

Read 2 Corinthians 5:17–21. Choose *one verse* from it and journal on it, using the SOAP acrostic at the end of the chapter. Take time to meditate on how you will live differently because of what you've just read.

> If anyone is in Christ, he is a new creature; the old things passed away; behold, new things have come.
>
> Now all these things are from God, who reconciled us to Himself through Christ and gave us the ministry of reconciliation, namely, that God was in Christ reconciling the world to Himself, not counting their trespasses against them, and He has committed to us the word of reconciliation.
>
> Therefore, we are ambassadors for Christ, as though God were making an appeal through us; we beg you on behalf of Christ, be reconciled to God.
>
> He made Him who knew no sin to be sin on our behalf, so that we might become the righteousness of God in Him.

Title:

// SCRIPTURE

// OBSERVATION

// APPLICATION

// PRAYER

12

The University of the Holy Spirit

It is written in the Prophets:
"They will all be taught by God."[1]

Your best friends will be found in the Bible. They are men and women who have been handpicked and ordained by God to befriend you. They will guide you and tutor you. No seminar, no conference, no leadership forum will outdo what you will learn from entering the Bible. To attempt a substitute is like parents allowing the media to raise their child.

Each year, as president of Pacific Rim Bible College here in Hawaii, I preside over our commencement ceremonies. The handing out of the diplomas is a joyous occasion for many, and, I suppose, a surprise to others!

Most of us plan to graduate from one institution or another; we set it as a goal. But there is one university we will never leave in this lifetime. This is the University of the Holy Spirit. The curriculum is a process of lifelong learning, coaching, and on-the-job training. Graduation will commence when we walk through heaven's gates. Until then, the University of the Holy Spirit will include studies, experiences, setbacks, consequences, disciplines, journeys, and a host of traveling companions.

Just this week I had the privilege of traveling for a few miles with one of our divine mentors. Ruth has taught me much through her humility and perseverance . . . two qualities I at times have sorely lacked. She recounted her story, and I recorded it, as I heard it, in the daily pages of my *Life Journal*.

A BEGGAR TURNED REGAL

The women said to Naomi: "Praise be to the Lord, who this day has not left you without a kinsman-redeemer. . . . Then Naomi took the child, laid him in her lap and cared for him. The women living there said, "Naomi has a son." And they named him Obed. He was the father of Jesse, the father of David. (Ruth 4:14,16–17 NIV)

OBSERVATION

There's no way she [Ruth] could have known. Not in a million years. Did she realize how closely her obedience would tie her to David, Israel's greatest king? Would she ever recognize how, through all the horrible circumstances, her "Kinsman-Redeemer" would be the Messiah? Could she ever comprehend how close she was to royalty when she was gleaning in Boaz's fields?

You can't see through to the future. Looking forward is often cloudy. Muddled. You fly blind. Except for one thing: obedience. It's like sonar. Obedience will not *remove* obstacles. It will only help you navigate through them. But it does have its requirements: Obedience compels us to live by trust and obedience, not by results and rewards. No preset guarantees. Only promises.

Ruth obeyed Naomi's instructions and kept herself chaste.

In an ancient world where begging women were not always connected with virtue, Ruth stands out. She remained true to God's instructions and her mother-in-law's intuition until Boaz recognized her faithfulness. "You have not run after the younger men, whether rich or poor."[2]

Obedience is recognizable.

APPLICATION

I wonder how many times I have been close to regal results but have bailed. I suspect many. But today, walking with Ruth, her counsel refreshed my soul. Her narration has stirred my heart.

Today I will reenlist in obedience. I seldom know in advance the outcomes of decisions made today. But still I will obey, regardless of what fears assail me.

Obedience is the guide to optimum futures, and today I have been fortunate. *I have had the opportunity to travel in the company of Ruth, a beggar turned regal.*

How heartening it is to have a friend recount an experience in her past so that I am emboldened to walk into the fullness of my future!

After walking with Ruth for those few miles, I paused and prayed this prayer:

PRAYER

Dear Father: I know You have my best interest at heart, and all You ask is that I be obedient, step by step. I renew my heart to You today. Please forgive me for the many times where I have balked and bailed. Thank You for Your patience toward such a surly saint as I. How grateful I am for Your obedience at Calvary when all of hell was against you. May I take heart today knowing that all of heaven is for me!

Look at John 5:39 (NLT): "You search the Scriptures because you believe they give you eternal life. But the Scriptures point to me!" Everything we learn directs us back to the Source.

The University of the Holy Spirit is much more than taking classes. It's not getting to know the information as much as it is getting to know the Informer!

A CLASS, OR A TUTOR?

Some time ago I took a class in jazz guitar at a local community college. Our excellent instructor taught us scales and chords that we would play together as a class.

But one student was a little slow. Often the teacher would interrupt his lesson with "Hold on, class," and he would walk over and individually instruct until the student learned to turn his guitar around, tune it correctly, and play the chords. This student basically held up the progress and speed of our class.

I really could have felt impatient about the whole situation, except for one fact.

I was that student.

Now, imagine if the legendary jazz guitarist Joe Pass had taught the class. When we finished for the day, suppose he approached me (the slow one) and said, "Wayne, I see a hint of promise in you as a young guitarist. I see some real potential. And I'd like to give you a choice: You can either remain in this once-a-week class, or I can meet with you every day for an hour. I will mentor you personally in jazz guitar. What do you think?"

Which do you think I would choose? Do you imagine I'd even need to mull it over? Not a chance!

I would instantly opt to be mentored by the renowned artist. I would say, "You tell me the time, and even if it's 2:00 A.M., I'll be there."

What an honor that would be.

No more than a year later, I suspect, someone would hear me play, stop in their tracks, and say, "*Where* did you learn *that*?"

"Oh," I'd explain, "I took a class at a community college."

They'd look at me sideways and reply, "Well, you may have, but that's not where you got *that*."

"What do you mean?"

"I can tell the difference. You didn't just take a class. Your phrasing, breathing, intonation, and voicing—I recognize those! That's the way Joe Pass plays. You don't get that from generic class instruction. You've been with the master. That's the only way you could learn to play that way."

And I'd admit it. "Yes, you're right. For the last year, I've been learning daily from Joe Pass himself."

There's a big difference between taking a class and being taught by the Master.

"I Hear Him in You!"

When you make daily devotions a habit—when you sit with the Spirit for at least forty minutes a day—a scenario like the one I just played out can actually happen to you. It won't be a year before you're sharing a prayer from your journal or describing an insight, and someone who's listening will stop you.

"Where did you get that revelation?" he or she will ask.

"Well, I went to Bible college."

"I'm sure you did, but it's a lot more than that. You didn't get that just by going to school. You were taught by the Master, weren't you? Flesh and blood didn't reveal that to you; my heavenly Father did."

What a difference!

The world won't be changed by those who take a weekly class. It will be changed by men and women who sit daily at the feet of Jesus, listening to His Word. Someone will hear you giving advice or offering counsel and they'll instantly recognize that your words have the tone of the Father's voice. They'll identify an authority and a resonance beyond you. And at that moment it won't be only you speaking; it will be the Father speaking through you. You will have actually become His spokesperson.

Keep Looking Forward!

// SCRIPTURE

*Do not call to mind the former things, or ponder things of
the past. Behold, I will do something new, now it will
spring forth; will you not be aware of it? I will even make
a roadway in the wilderness, rivers in the desert.*

(Isaiah 43:18–19)

// OBSERVATION

Isaiah reminds me today to *keep looking forward.* "What's next?" should be the
cry of my heart. "What can I repair or develop in order to improve? What must I
correct, refocus, prepare for? In what shall I invest my time?"

// APPLICATION

Polishing trophies and pondering mistakes can both rob me of my future.
Although accolades are nice, I must, as Paul instructs, forget what lies behind and
press forward to what lies ahead (see Philippians 3:13–14). It's in what's ahead
that potential is found, promise is discovered, hope is uncovered, expectations are
released, and vision is fashioned.

Only when I begin to look forward will I see the roadways in the wilderness and
the rivers in the desert. Pondering the past will leave me blind.

Rehearsing my hurts or licking my wounds will also steal my tomorrows. I will
grab the lessons, thank "Consequences" for its brutal but effective teaching
method, and then move forward to better my future. As C. S. Lewis said, "When
you keep your face toward the sun, the shadows will always fall behind you."

// PRAYER

Thank You, Lord Jesus, for increasing my potential by redirecting my
focus and for opening my eyes to rivers and roadways I had not seen before.

Not a Program but a Process

That's a life-changing, eternity-impacting difference. It's the difference between someone saying to you, "Excuse me, but are you by any chance a Christian?" and "Wow! You sound just like Jesus. Who taught you that?"

When you start sitting at the Lord's feet and listening to His Word, repeatedly running what you've heard through your mind, eventually His thoughts become your thoughts and His ways become your ways. And then you will start to put on what the Bible calls "the mind of Christ."[3]

Once again:

> When they saw the courage of Peter and John and realized that they were unschooled, ordinary men, they were astonished and they took note that these men had been with Jesus.[4]

How can you respond to life's twists and turns the way Jesus himself would respond? The only way is by learning to think as He thinks. When that happens, you'll begin to respond the way He responds.

The more you continue to read Scripture, the more you begin to think as He thinks and act as He acts. And that's how, over time, you gain the wisdom of the ages. In fact, you might say that every time you read the Bible, God inspires it anew.

The Invitation Is Ours to Accept or Deny

The Lord is asking each of us the same question and extending to us the same invitation: *Are you going to choose to feed yourself, rather than waiting to be spoon-fed once a week? Will you choose to enter the University of the Spirit, where I can personally mentor you daily?*

What an honor to be personally mentored by God himself, every single day! And as you spend prayerful time in His Word, that's exactly what takes place. But notice I said *prayerful* time. If you come to the Bible daily for twenty hours of intensive study and yet do not invite God to interact with you through its pages, then you'll be climbing in the same boat that took Judas Iscariot so far off the charted course.

All the disciples, including Judas, had been with the Master every day for three solid years, but not until after Pentecost did most of the lessons they'd heard get applied to their hearts. Why the delay? Because at Pentecost God sent the Holy Spirit to indwell each believer, in part to drive the lessons they'd heard deep into their hearts. It *must* be the Divine Mentor applying the lessons of Scripture to our hearts; else we end up acquiring useless knowledge, esoteric facts, and biblical trivia.

Remember, Judas spent essentially as much time in the presence of Jesus as the other disciples. Yes, Peter, James, and John got some special tutoring time. But Judas had been at the side of God's Son for months on end, watching miracle after miracle, hearing teaching after teaching.

Judas threw it all overboard.

MISSING THE POINT

F. Kefa Sempangi's great book called *A Distant Grief* alerts us to the fact that we can miss the point. Sempangi endured Idi Amin's horrific dictatorship during Uganda's oppressive past. As a young minister, he witnessed the persecutions and slayings of many believers. His friends would disappear, and whole villages were massacred. To escape the maltreatment, he fled with his family to the United States.

There he and his wife, Penina, enrolled in a seminary to further train for ministry. As time passed, so did the constant fears they'd lived under for years. The tensions and anxieties that had become the norm of their existence slowly became a thing of the past, and they began to have a new calm and security.

Sempangi writes:

Our first semester passed quickly. Penina gave birth to our son, Duwudi Bubumba. In the fall, I returned to my studies. It was then, in my second year, that I noticed the change that had come into my life. In Uganda, Penina and I read the Bible for hope and life. We read to hear God's promises, to hear His commands and obey them. There had been no time for argument and no time for religious discrepancies or doubts.

Now, in the security of a new life and with the reality of death fading from mind, I found myself reading the Scripture to analyze texts and speculate about meaning. I came to enjoy abstract theological discussions with my fellow students and, while these discussions were intellectually refreshing, it wasn't long before our fellowship revolved around ideas rather than the work of God in our lives. It was not the blood of Jesus Christ that gave us unity, but our agreement on doctrinal issues. We came together not for confession and forgiveness, but for debate.[5]

We cannot miss the point. It is not the program but the process that changes our hearts as we sit with the Master. This is not an end in itself but a means to the likeness and the mind of Christ. Look closely to see *Him,* not to snag information about Him. Listen for His voice, not for a new idea. Catch the heart of God, and be slow to espouse new information until it bleeds out your toes. Let it sink in first. It's food for your soul before it's fodder for your ideas.

THE HIGHEST FORM OF PRAYER

Years ago I attended a high-octane Pentecostal prayer meeting in Portland, Oregon. I was a brand-new Christian, only three weeks old in the Lord. This church was well known for meetings that started at 7:00 P.M. and lasted all night long. It was a loud cacophony of sound, with everyone praying in a spiritual language and crying at the top of their voices.

To me, it sounded really spiritual.

I thought the "winner" would be the one who talked the loudest, fastest, and most—without breathing—for a solid hour.

But I left that night deeply discouraged. I couldn't pray like that. I had to breathe now and again! And that meant they beat me.

What an excuse for a Christian I am, I thought.

As I walked home, though, another thought occurred to me: *Now, wait a minute. If they're talking solidly for one hour, then when do they listen for His voice? I think I need to hear what God is saying to me a whole lot more than He needs to hear what I'm saying to Him. There has to be a better way to pray. But then . . . what do I know? I'm only a new believer.*

I continued to walk and think about it more, and eventually some conclusions began forming in my brain. *Okay . . . when I'm reading the Bible, who's talking? God. And who's listening? Me. So then—does that mean the highest form of prayer is when I'm doing my devotions and God is talking to me?*

I believe I hit the nail on the head.

Make no mistake: *The highest form of prayer is not you talking to God. It's Him talking to you.*

MORE ONE WAY THAN TWO

Yes, I realize there is supplication. There is intercession. There is thanksgiving and praise. But none of that is *ever* a substitute for sitting at His feet and listening to His Word with a wide-open heart and ears straining to hear every word. I am convinced that we need to hear more from God than He needs to hear from us. We need to hear more of His plans for our lives than He needs to hear about our plans for the future.

A friend recently told me, "Wayne, so often I read the Word but don't take time for prayer. I think, *I don't have time for that.* I manage to find time to read the Word so I can make a check mark on my spiritual to-do list. I honestly do! But I'm finding that the best course corrections come when I'm on my face before God, waiting on Him. That's when He really starts explaining things to me."

Listen! Did you hear that? Another hammer hitting another nail. We receive our best instruction, not when we're talking, but when we're listening.

Think of David, a favorite mentor for us all. Yet he didn't always listen for God's voice, did he? Before he committed adultery with Bathsheba, how many times do you think the Lord rang a bell of warning? I'll bet it was time and time again. But David refused to listen, hardened his heart, and finally sank to the gross sins of illicit sex and murder.

We have to soften our hearts, willingly, and make them more susceptible to the warning bells and urgent calls of our Father who loves us. When your heart is open before Him, it becomes very susceptible even to His whispers; God no longer needs to shout.

Believe me, my friend, it's a lot better to listen for divine whispers than to wait for a divine shout. Usually those shouts come in the form of serious consequences—and you just don't need that.

What might that "listening" look like?

Maybe it means getting up from your Bible reading and prayer time and taking a little walk, inviting God's Spirit to speak to you, to apply the truth you just read.

Maybe it means jotting down a verse that God highlighted in your devotions—putting it on a three-by-five card or Post-it note and sticking it in your pocket or purse. Then, several times during the day, pulling that bit of truth from your pocket and asking the Divine Mentor to speak to you through those words.

Maybe it's taking a lunch break alone and reviewing what you've written in your journal over the past few weeks.

Whatever the specifics, *the essential ingredients here are the Word of God, the Spirit of God, and a heart that strains to hear God's voice.*

TRULY HONORING THE KING

Do you remember the touching story of how three of David's mighty men risked their lives to fulfill an impetuous whim of their leader? I think this account can teach us a lot about true worship.

At the time, Israel's traditional enemies, the Philistines, controlled David's hometown of Bethlehem. One day, while David and his men rested in a rocky stronghold, David absentmindedly said to no one in particular, "Oh, that someone would get me a drink of water from the well near the gate of Bethlehem!"[6]

I don't think he meant for anyone to take him seriously. He may not even have realized anyone was listening. He was just expressing a longing for a drink of the pure, cold water for which Bethlehem was famous. A musing at best. A wish tossed into the air.

Three of his men heard the offhand request, looked at each other, and quietly slipped out of the stronghold. Sneaking through the Philistine lines, they somehow managed to grab a cup of water from the well and make their way back to David.

When they arrived in the stronghold, they held out the cup of precious liquid to their leader and said, "You know that special drink you wanted? Well, here it is!"

David looked up in shock. The loyalty, courage, and daring of his men shook him to the core. He gingerly took the cup, but instead of drinking it, he basically said, "I'm not worthy of this! You men risked your lives to retrieve it, but I can't accept such an extravagant gift." So do you know what he did? He knelt down and poured out the water before the Lord, thus saying through his actions, "This is worthy only of worship to the King of Kings."

When I read that story, David dropped a new insight into my heart, one for which I've been ever so grateful. I wrote in my *Life Journal* these words:

The Musings of a King

// SCRIPTURE

So the three broke through the camp of the Philistines
and drew water from the well of Bethlehem which was by
the gate, and took it and brought it to David; nevertheless
David would not drink it, but poured it out to the Lord;
and he said, "Be it far from me before my God that I
should do this. Shall I drink the blood of these men who
went at the risk of their lives? For at the risk of their lives
they brought it . . . Therefore he would not drink it. These
things the three mighty men did.
(1 Chronicles 11:18–19)

// OBSERVATION

David didn't have to shout at his men to go and bring the water. He didn't command them to bring it. He simply mused about it. Just the musings of the king, even the very suggestion of the king, was enough to motivate these men to action.

// APPLICATION

That kind of faith action is the epitome of honor, and the fruit of that labor is worthy for only One, the Lord of Lords. There is no higher worship than to be able to recognize the heart sighs of the King, and that is sufficient to move me to exploits, to take risks, to break through the lines the enemy has drawn.

How often I wait for a shout, but that does not please the King. It would require no faith on my part if He shouted. I often wait for the hammer to fall before I move. That brings no pleasure. Yet I lift my voice in rapture to the latest worship chorus that hits the charts, and I call that worship.

Instead, worship at its highest level is developing my heart to such a level of sensitivity that even the musings of my King are enough to move me to action. There is nothing greater.

// PRAYER

Father, may I be so close to You that I can hear Your musings and be moved to action!

It's the whispered longings from the heart of our God that must be enough to motivate me to action. It may *include* the singing of choruses, but it is far greater than that.

Worship begins with my daily times before His throne, listening to His heart. And, when I leave, I expect to live differently because of what I just heard. It is often a whisper you will hear from the King . . . but if you will follow it through, you will hear a shout from heaven. There is nothing that delights Him more.

A Final Word:
The Presence
of God

What else will distinguish me and
your people from all the other people
on the face of the earth?[1]

Allow me to explain what is probably the greatest benefit of being permeated by God's Word on a daily basis.

Hawaii has a special allure. The beautiful climate and gentle trade winds give the islands a unique appeal that brings over a hundred thousand visitors each month to their tropical shores. Charming nights, balmy mornings, and an effervescent ocean give this Pacific state its nickname: "Paradise." There's just no better place than Hawaii!

However, for me personally, Hawaii's greatest charm is its people. It seems as if anyone with any amount of Polynesian blood in him can sing, dance, or conquer the waves with a surfboard. Unpretentious and without airs, these warm people have a flair for disguising remarkable talent with simplicity and grace.

Some of the world's best musicians, artisans, and sportsmen come clothed as modest citizens. An unassuming mother of four will surface out of a crowd of picnickers to solo with ukulele a beautiful Hawaiian lullaby that will stir your soul.

Another will dance, and yet another will play an instrumental with his guitar tuned in a special pitch called a "slack key."

Most unassuming of all are "the water people." These are a special athletic breed. Many have been raised near the shores, where daily contact with the ocean is as natural as breathing air. That was the case with "Nappy."

Joseph "Nappy" Napoleon is a legend. Sixty-three years old, Nappy is one of Hawaiian canoe racing's patriarchs. He balances a strong competitive drive with a laid-back, friendly approach. Knowledgeable paddlers rightly look at him with great respect. His many accomplishments as a paddler and able steersman have found him no equal in open-ocean competition. He has participated in the annual forty-two mile inter-island competition more than fifty times. He seems to know each wave by name and is more comfortable in the water than he is on land.

I met Nappy a few years ago when I took up the sport. He was like a celebrity to me. Tanned by the sun and accentuated by his Hawaiian heritage, he was easy to recognize. It was my first race. I showed up with a new paddle, new board shorts, and a top-brand shirt I'd purchased on sale. (I figured if I couldn't win, I'd at least look good in the process!)

Nappy arrived like he'd just come from working in his yard. His paddle, which looked as if it doubled as a garden tool, was old and chipped. He wore faded shorts and a T-shirt that advertised a local restaurant. He got there just before the race began. No water bottle, no power gels, and no protein bar. He merely showed up . . . alone!

When we crossed the finish line, I noticed him again. His crew had already arrived twenty minutes before ours. He was on the shore enjoying a cool drink, watching our exhausted canoe plow its way homeward, contending for second-to-last place.

It was said that Nappy had "the touch." From years of experience and hundreds of races, he just had it in him. I guess when you've got it within you, you don't need all the trim-mings. He said the embellishments and trappings only slowed him down.

And he was right. "The touch" was worth far more than all the accessories I'd purchased.

THE HAND OF GOD

David was like that. The scrawny shepherd boy didn't have much. In fact, it was in one of his earlier contests that Saul's armor was offered to him. I'm sure the king had the latest in protective fashion: light, strong, yet flexible for even the most demanding of warriors. David rejected it. A well-worn leather sling and a few smooth stones were enough to bring down the giant who'd been taunting Israel. David had the touch, and when God's touch was upon him, not much stood in his way.

Everything else would just slow him down.

Ezra was like that too. He was an Old Testament "Nappy," distinguished from others as one upon whom the Lord's hand rested.

> Ezra . . . was a scribe skilled in the law of Moses, which the Lord God of Israel had given; and the king granted him all he requested because the hand of the Lord his God was upon him.[2]

This seasoned saint confessed that God had "extended loving-kindness to me. . . . Thus I was strengthened according to the hand of the Lord my God upon me."[3]

Ezra had the touch, and wherever he went, God worked with him in powerful ways.

A DISTINGUISHING MARK

Old Testament stories talk about the Shekinah, God's glory, which led the children of Israel through the Sinai. A cloud by day and a pillar of fire by night manifested the Lord's divine presence.[4] That presence, though it brought the people confidence in victory, had an even greater role: It's what distinguished them from every other people on the face of the earth.

When God threatened to remove His presence, Moses pleaded with Him:

> If Your presence does not go with us, do not lead us up from here. For how then can it be known that I have found favor in Your sight, I and Your people? Is it not by Your going with us, so that we, I and Your people, may be distinguished from all the other people who are upon the face of the earth?[5]

What sets God's people apart from everyone else is not our accoutrements or our language. It won't be our music, our programs, or our bumper stickers. It will be the presence of the Lord . . . His hand being upon us.

For years I've been an avid student of "the hand of God." Sometimes I've watched His hand rest on certain people and ministries and remain there for decades. Other times I've seen Him remove His hand from one ministry and set it down on another. I've also observed the aftermath of a ministry that once enjoyed His touch but now was bereft of His hand. That ministry no longer exists.

My greatest fear is not of falling away from God. It isn't losing my marriage or reverting back to drugs. My greatest fear is that I should ever lose God's hand on my life. Without His touch, everything I would do, as Solomon said, would be "vanity of vanities!"[6]

Anointed With Gladness

// SCRIPTURE

> You have loved righteousness and hated lawlessness;
> therefore God, Your God, has anointed You with the oil of
> gladness more than Your companions. (Hebrews 1:9 NKJV
> from Psalm 45:7)

// OBSERVATION

This reminds us of the source of gladness! It's *not* simply being giddy. It's *not* a positive mindset reminding ourselves to be happy. Rather, it is a God-given "anointing." He himself will place a special dispensation of deep, lasting gladness upon those who *love righteousness and hate lawlessness.*

The word for "lawlessness" means "ungovernable." This is the inability or unwillingness to be governed. The inability to be corrected and brought under submission. It's like a mustang that refuses the bridle. It's a life that refuses to be placed under supervision or discipline. This morphs into an unteachable heart.

Gladness is the result of a life willingly submitted to disciplines that will produce fruit.

// APPLICATION

I must love righteousness, for it produces an abiding confidence and a satisfaction in my soul. Gladness comes not only from doing what is right but also from *loving* to do it. It's an anointing of gladness, not merely a sporadic happiness.

// PRAYER

Father, this is something I'd very much like to experience! Please anoint me with gladness. I will be one who loves righteousness and hates lawlessness. Help me to remain teachable and submitted to those You have placed in my life to coach, guide, and direct me.

PETITIONING FOR HIS HAND

Elisha petitioned for a double portion of Elijah's spirit. He didn't wait around for a possibility of it happening. He asked for it, he geared up for it, and he was willing to steward his petition should it be granted. Can we appeal for the Lord's hand? Can we plead for His favor?

Moses did.

Moses said to the Lord, "You have been telling me, 'Lead these people,' but you have not let me know whom you will send with me. . . . If you are pleased with me, teach me your ways so I may know you and continue to find favor with you. Remember that this nation is your people." The Lord replied, "My Presence will go with you."[7]

Moses hadn't gone this way before. He needed a Guide, but God had not yet let him know whom else He would send. He needed a mentor, a coach, a guide.

God said He would send His Spirit, or presence, in the form of the Shekinah. In the New Testament, Jesus calls His Spirit the Helper: "I will ask the Father, and He will give you another Helper, that He may be with you forever."[8] The literal word translated "Helper" is *Paraclétos* (English: Paraclete), meaning "the one called alongside to help."

God offers a Helper to escort us through life. There is no greater Guide, no more knowledgeable a Teacher, no more discerning a Counselor. Divine mentorship is available to each one who will petition His hand.

"I know the plans that I have for you," declares the Lord, "plans for welfare and not for calamity to give you a future and a hope."[9]

Jeremiah 29:11 is my life verse. I have always been thankful that God has divinely preplanned my future. I have to admit, though, that I'm not always able to see those plans. If I can't see them, I may not be able to walk in them. Right?

Wrong.

I was a high school pastor for ten years before moving back to Hawaii. One of my annual highlights was high school summer camp. Being a kid at heart, that week gave me an excuse to let my hair down (I had more of it back then) and enjoy life!

One of our practices was to wake the kids at twelve on the second night and take them on a midnight hike. Groggy from sleep shortage the first night, they'd stumble out of bed mumbling something about their parents paying good money for this. But to the staff this was crucial: We had to establish the rules of order so that they'd obey the rules the rest of the week.

Lined up in the open field, they looked like tired Ewoks. We'd weave them, single file, through a preplanned route, with one catch: Only the leaders had flashlights. We knew where we were going, and the kids didn't have a clue.

This was intentional—we did it to keep them near us! Their whole goal would be to stay near to those who knew the way. What they didn't know was that we were taking them on a roundabout route to a crackling campfire, with s'mores and hot chocolate waiting.

FOLLOWING THE GUIDE

In this life, we might know that God has a plan, but like those young hikers, we're often in the dark. There *is* One, nonetheless, who knows the way. He is our Divine Mentor, and He knows every inch of this divinely ordained route. Note where He entered the picture:

> In the beginning God created the heavens and the earth. The earth was formless and void, and darkness was over the surface of the deep; and the *Spirit of God* was moving over the surface of the waters.[10]

The Spirit is introduced in the Bible's very first book, first chapter, second verse! In other words, He was there before time even began. Before we were created and before God wrote down His plans for my future, the Holy Spirit was there! So He knows my future. He knows where I'm supposed to end up. He knows what I'm supposed to become. He knows all the divine plans, and not only that . . .

He knows the way!

I may not know what my future holds, but I do know who holds that future, so my goal in life is to stay near the Guide. I don't know the way, but the Spirit does! He was with God in the divine design room for all the preplanning.

"We are His workmanship, created in Christ Jesus for good works, which God prepared beforehand so that we would walk in them" says Paul.[11] The Lord designed us deliberately intended for good works, and He means for us to carry them out. That's why He's assigned us a Helper, our Divine Mentor, to tutor us into our inheritance.

The best thing I can do for myself is keep a close relationship with the One who knows the way. He will take me through the darkness and to His best. He designed it that way, because He knew if He didn't, I'd be off on my own, aimlessly exploring dead-end rabbit trails and finding myself in ditches.

I will stay close to the Guide, and my daily times with God draw me close.

THE ULTIMATE DIFFERENCE

I have seen that the people who stay close to the Helper are the same people who have God's touch on their lives. His hand is on them. They may look like average citizens, but in reality they're far from average.

Astronomers say we're traveling at over sixty-six thousand miles an hour on a rotating globe that's spinning on a twenty-three-and-a-half-degree tilt. We're spinning faster than the spin cycle on our washing machine! And we don't have much time left—a few more spins and we'll be done. The psalmist reminds us that our life is but a breath.[12] James calls the duration a "vapor."[13]

We have only so much time left to become what God planned for us to become. To increase activity in the wrong direction makes everything futile. We need a Guide!

Read again what Moses said to Him:

> If your Presence does not go with us, do not send us up from here. How will anyone know that you are pleased with me and with your people unless you go with us? What else will distinguish me and your people from all the other people on the face of the earth?[14]

My final word to you: Do everything you possibly can to integrate the lessons of this book into the very fabric of your life. It's not theory—it's tried and true.

All the mentors of the ages await your audience. Don't keep them waiting. Enter the Bible daily, and there will be a dusting of heaven on everything you do.

That is what will distinguish us from all the other peoples of the world, more than any other trimming or trappings.

Those will only slow you down.

Appendix:
Frequently Asked
Questions

B elow are the most frequently asked questions posed to me about journaling. Should you have others, please e-mail them to info@lifejournal.cc.

(1) WHY SHOULD I JOURNAL?

Some people say, "Wayne, I read the Bible, but I don't journal. Should I journal?"

"Yes."

"Why?"

Well, partly because in the book of Deuteronomy, God required Israel's kings to write out all of His Word in their own handwriting, then read, every day, what they had written. He mandated this practice, He says, so that the hearts of the kings might not be lifted up above their fellowman and would not become prideful.

Now, as I said earlier in the book, if God made this a daily requirement of Israel's kings, then I think it's not too much to ask of the King's kids. Regular, prayerful time in the Bible keeps our hearts from straying.

How about other reasons? I listed a few in chapter 6. (See, for instance, under "Honoring God With Our Note-Taking.")

For one thing, journaling will help you when the tests come—and they *will*.

Also, as a communicator, I counsel people to journal because I know that the more you learn to write, the better your communication will be. You become better able to take tangled thoughts and articulate them. You develop the ability to compose your feelings and ideas in an effective and powerful way. When you're called upon to stand and speak, you'll be able to communicate more effectively because you've learned to write.

Sir Francis Bacon once said, "Reading maketh a full man; conference maketh a ready man; and writing maketh an exact man." Today, we'd say that writing makes us more precise thinkers.

As you write, you become a wordsmith: "Hmm, this adjective doesn't work; this adverb is better; this turn of a phrase is better." Writing teaches you to do it on the fly. One practical serendipity is that one day, when you begin to speak extemporaneously, you'll also start to wordsmith on the fly. You'll say in your head, *This phrase works better than that, and this is better than the other.* In nanoseconds, you're wordsmithing. The regular practice of journaling will be a tremendous help in developing your communication skills.

(2) WHICH BIBLE TRANSLATION SHOULD I USE?

I don't make much fuss over the particular translation someone uses. I just want him or her to regularly use it! Of course, you don't want one that calls itself *The New World Translation*—that's a faulty version created by a cult. Only make sure that you have a translation you can understand.

You'll find a number of good paraphrases—*The Living Bible, The Message,* or *Good News for Modern Man*—renderings that seek to take the Bible's message and translate it into English idea for idea (rather than word for word).

The late Ken Taylor created *The Living Bible* when he wanted a version his grandchildren could understand. At that time there were very few English translations available. Taylor's work was like a breath of fresh air. A newer translation called the *New Living Translation* builds on and fine-tunes his work. I think it's excellent.

Other versions try to translate more word for word than idea for idea: some of the popular ones include the *New American Standard Bible*, the *King James Version*, and the *New King James Version*. Somewhere in the middle is a translation like the *New International Version* (which has been the top-selling English Bible for many years). The NIV reads at about an eighth-grade level, using vocabulary, phraseology, grammar, and syntax most Americans can easily understand.

Choose whichever translation fits best for you. Whatever you choose, *get to know this Book!* Get to know it with all your heart. Choose to regularly sit at the Lord's feet and listen to His Word.

(3) WHAT'S WRONG WITH USING OTHER BOOKS FOR MY DEVOTIONS?

Some people say to me, "I do my daily devotions, but I read *My Utmost for His Highest* or *Our Daily Bread*. What's wrong with using books like these? Aren't they based on the Bible?"

To that I say, "There is only one book in the universe God promised to inspire; it's not by J. Oswald Chambers, and I'll bet Chambers himself wouldn't find any argument with that statement! The only book the Lord has pledged to inspire is the one that Paul, in Ephesians 6, calls the sword of the Spirit.

Of course, this is not an either/or thing—it's a both/and! But first and foremost, you need to go directly to the Word itself for God-breathed instruction. That's what *inspiration* means: "God-breathed."

The Bible has stood the test of time. Other volumes may be classics that remain popular for a hundred years or even a thousand. The Bible has endured from the start, and its end will never come. We simply have to get back to the Bible.

(4) WHY IS IT SO IMPORTANT TO DO DEVOTIONS EVERY DAY?

Let's change the question a bit. What if God traded out our eyes for His? What if, by divine dispensation, we were allowed to see things through *His* eyes . . . to see, not as man sees, but as He sees? What if we were granted a momentary metamorphosis and saw people's true, spiritual condition? Would we be heartbroken or heart-lifted at what we saw? Sad or surprised? In anguish or in awe?

What if we could see, not how we look to one another, but how we look to God? What would happen if we could pray, in faith, a prayer like that of Elisha regarding his servant?

> "O Lord, I pray, open his eyes that he may see." And the Lord opened the servant's eyes and he saw; and behold, the mountain was full of horses and chariots of fire all around Elisha.[1]

What would the people in your church look like if they snacked on meager food morsels during the week and ate only one good meal on the weekend? You know the answer, don't you? You'd find yourself surrounded by emaciated, gaunt people in desperate need of nutrition.

And how would these undernourished believers fare against a demonic adversary? Can you imagine how this army would look? You'd see threadbare skeletons with hollow cheeks and sunken eye-sockets, lined up like phantoms. Weakened by famine, that shriveled militia could barely stand at attention; each would struggle to find the strength to keep his or her bony frame upright.

Could this "army" conquer an opposing force?

No way. No earthly general would send them out to fight.

Well, then, how about the army of the Lord? What of those who gather on Sunday mornings? Are they spiritually nourished to fight the battles ahead? Considering what most members of God's army subsist on—an occasional tidy snack from a devotional book and perhaps an average-sized meal on Sundays to satiate conscience—you'd have to conclude that God's fighting force has some serious training to do.

Have you ever wondered why marriages seemingly crumble overnight, and—out of the blue—Christians leaders fall to luring temptations?

The truth is, no marriage *instantly* disintegrates, and no one *suddenly* falls away from Christ. For that matter, no one dies from an eating disorder after missing a day or two of meals.

It could better be described as a slow decline—gradual spiritual starvation, barely even discernible to the outside observer. The malnourishment of God's sons and daughters happens over time, as they eat less and less. Then, in their weakness, they do something that shocks everyone, finally revealing what was really going on in their spiritual lives.

Did you know that more than 80 percent of those who call themselves Christians read their Bibles only once a week? And that's usually on Sundays, at church. They come to church to get their spiritual fill, and then snack on devotional tidbits for the rest of the week (if even that).

I wish for just one day God would change the way our eyes work, so we would see ourselves spiritually. We'd see most American churches filled with skeletal, hollow-eyed saints, looking as if a gust of wind would blow them away like tumbleweeds.

Which is why, when some new trend floods America and pushes our nation further away from God, further away from our spiritual roots, the church is unable to withstand the tide. We simply don't have the strength.

So what's the solution?

As I mentioned earlier, the *American Journal of Medicine* recently published a highly revealing conclusion: The health of twenty-first-century America will no longer be determined by what people can get doctors to do for them but by what doctors can get people to do for themselves.

Do you see how this prescription applies equally to the church? If we eat only once a week, it's no wonder the church is weak and struggling. But daily fresh bread can change all of that. Regularly dining on fresh bread makes for a stalwart, strong, developed army—the only kind of force that will always make a difference in this world.

(5) BUT WHAT IF I JUST DON'T HAVE THE TIME?

Sometimes even though we know reading the Bible is important, we don't think we have the time to do it regularly. So many things are happening in our lives—we are just too busy! We'd like to feast on God's Word, but when will we have the time?

Here's what I say to that: "We will *always* have time for the things we see as important and enjoyable."

If we think golf is important, we find time to play. We might feel listless and tired on a Sunday morning, in no mood to attend a boring church service—but if a friend invites us to try out a new course, we'll find the energy.

Because we always have time for the things we enjoy and consider important, what does it say to us if we claim we simply can't find forty minutes a day to spend alone with God?

(6) SOME PASSAGES ARE DIFFICULT TO UNDERSTAND. WHAT IF I ONLY UNDERSTAND TEN PERCENT?

You're not alone in this. Peter understood exactly what you're going through. Listen to these words:

> This is what our beloved brother Paul also wrote to you with the wisdom God gave him—speaking of these things in all of his letters. *Some of his comments are hard to understand.*[2]

I love that. If Peter had a tough time, we certainly don't

need to be wound up about not comprehending everything. However, we don't end there. I mentioned this earlier in the book: If you don't understand 90 percent, then don't get tied up about what you may be "missing" this time around. Journal on the 10 percent you *do* understand.

Be faithful with what God reveals to you. When you are, next time around, you will understand 20 percent . . . then 40 percent . . . then 60 percent. Obeying what you do understand is crucial to receiving future revelation. If I don't apply the truths I do understand, why should the Lord reveal to me truths I don't yet understand?

And here's a great prayer for when you begin reading the Scriptures. David taught me this one, and the same is offered to you.

> Open my eyes, that I may behold
> Wonderful things from Your law.[3]

He will.

(7) I've Heard That the King James Version Is the Only Anointed English Translation of the Bible. Is This True?

No. There are many wonderful versions and paraphrases of the Bible. (See also under Question 2.) In broad terms, a *version* has been translated, word for word, from the Bible's original languages. A *paraphrase* is taken from a version and is presented "idea for idea."

Among the various versions, the *New International* is very well-loved. Most people read at around an eighth-grade level. The relatively easy to understand NIV has positioned itself into that category. *The New King James Version* is listed at a ninth-grade level, and the *New American Standard Version* is rendered at an eleventh-grade level. These are more accurate on the verb tenses but sometimes a bit harder to read.

The *King James* is rated at a twelfth-grade level. It was not in print until 1611, and Paul the apostle was beheaded in Rome around AD 66, so obviously he didn't use it. He also didn't read English but rather Greek, Hebrew, and Aramaic.

Among the paraphrases, several are excellent, including *The Message* and *Good News for Modern Man*. As you begin, you may find one more suitable to your style than another. A brand-new believer may settle on a paraphrase at first, then move to a translation later.

Regardless, the bottom line is that you read the Bible!

(8) WHAT IF I MISS A DAY OR TWO?

Do not be discouraged! When you get back to your schedule, begin with the present day's reading. Do not go back to where you left off and attempt to motor your way back. Start with today's reading and hear what God is saying to you. Then, should you have some extra time, go back and revisit the days you missed. If it's several weeks, I suggest you simply pick up with today's reading and, next year, you'll go back over the territory you missed.

Refuse condemnation. Reject discouragement and guilt. We're all growing and developing godly habits. Don't induce fault, remorse, or a sense of failure into your discipline.

Only joy!

(9) HOW LONG DOES THE JOURNALING TIME TAKE?

We have implemented a 20/20/20 method (see chapter 10). That's twenty minutes for reading, followed by twenty minutes for journaling, and then, in a group setting, twenty minutes to share together what we've written in our journals. The whole life group takes, on the average, one hour. If you're doing devotions alone, this same equation works, except for the sharing portion. Then you can complete your devotions in forty minutes.

(10) IF IT'S A LARGE GROUP, NOT EVERYONE WILL HAVE TIME TO SHARE. WHAT DO WE DO THEN?

Some of my groups have included up to forty people. In fact, I've had some up to two hundred. A larger gathering is not a problem.

After our twenty minutes of reading and twenty minutes of journaling, I have the group break into smaller clusters of threes or fours, and they read their journals to one another. Then, when we've concluded, I may read mine and give commentary on it. Or I'll ask the group to volunteer someone to share insights. You'll always have eager and willing friends to volunteer one another!

(11) I'VE USUALLY DONE MY DEVOTIONS ALONE. SHOULDN'T THIS BE A PRIVATE TIME BETWEEN JUST ME AND THE LORD?

Remember, I'm *not* suggesting a type of classic Bible study group where one person teaches and everybody listens to his or her stories and commentary.

In the life group, for your first forty minutes, no one talks! The Holy Spirit is mentoring you. You're alone with Him even though there are others around you. Each person is "shut in" with the Lord.

The final twenty minutes, though, is also for listening and learning. So many times I've had moments of revelation through someone else's journal entry. So often I've come away richer for having been with others who are hearing from God. I've never felt intruded upon as I've sat in my "secret place" with the Most High.

(12) I'VE TRIED TO GET MY PASTOR TO BUY INTO THE LIFE JOURNAL, BUT HE SAYS HE HAS HIS OWN PLAN. I GET SO FRUSTRATED. WHAT SHOULD I DO?

No one method is the right one or the only one. Although I've taken twenty years to simplify, test, and improve our devotions, this is still by no means the only way. My suggestion is that you start with you and a few others with whom you'd like to meet. Enjoy it, savor it, and watch how God uses it to transform your life. Let the Spirit increase it to include more and more people. But *start deep, not fast.*

(13) CAN WE TAKE THE LIFE JOURNAL AND CHANGE IT?

The *Life Journal* is copyrighted and may not be changed, but you can have custom journals printed for your church with permission (see Question 14, below). The Bible-Reading Program is designed to help you read through the Old Testament once and the New Testament twice each year. We ask churches to use it but not change it or tout it as a devotional requirement.

Of course you may make any reading plan you like, but this one was designed so that even if people from different churches or denominations gather, they'll all be on the same page and be reading the same passages. This is for the sake of unity and fellowship, camaraderie, and solidarity. If each church develops its own, then only the people from that congregation will be able to read together. I had one life group in which people from five different churches gathered. We all had such a fantastic time in the Word and in fellowship!

(14) WHERE CAN WE OBTAIN LIFE JOURNALS?

You may order them from *www.lifejournal.cc.*

(15) WHAT IF I DON'T HAVE THE MONEY TO BUY A LIFE JOURNAL?

We don't have a problem with spending money. We do it every day. We spend the equivalent of a journal for one meal in a fast-food restaurant.

Investing in your growth in Christ is the greatest investment you can make. When you think about it, many of us spend more on an evening movie ticket than we do on what may bring eternal dividends! Don't get duped by the myth that something like spiritual growth should cost you nothing.

I can hear my friend David calling from the other room. He's reminding us of his words to Ornan: "I will not take what is yours . . . or offer a burnt offering which costs me nothing."[4]

The person who doesn't buy a journal in order to save money is like a person who unplugs the clock to save time.

Learn to invest in your personal growth with Christ. There is no higher venture.

(16) IF I CANNOT GET A LIFE JOURNAL, WHERE DO I BEGIN?

One suggestion is to purchase a notebook and set it up like a *Life Journal.* Leave the first page for your table of contents and the second for a prayer list. Then begin numbering your daily pages from the third page.

For headings, have your table of contents include "Date," "Scripture," "Title," and "Page" across the top. You could also copy the reading schedule from a *Life Journal* and tape it into your journal. When you've completed these steps, you're ready to go!

(17) WHAT IF SOMEONE SHARES HIS OR HER JOURNAL AND IT'S THEOLOGICALLY IN "OUTER SPACE"?

Do not fear. This gives you a great opportunity to practice your people skills by showing graciousness in leadership. Paul reminds us of this:

> Brethren, even if anyone is caught in any trespass, you who are spiritual, restore such a one in a spirit of gentleness; each one looking to yourself, so that you too will not be tempted.[5]

As Christians, we need open forums to discuss differing perspectives, and some of those perspectives may be very differing! Discuss them and reason together. The Holy Spirit will be there to help, and should you end up in an argument, take it before someone who may be more advanced in wisdom, and/or take time to research it. In the end, you'll all be wiser and more knowledgeable.

However, *remember to resolve the issue without forfeiting relationships.* Never exchange a healthy friendship for a "win" in an apologetic battle. It isn't worth it. The body of Christ is replete with unresolved theological battles: for instance, "Once Saved, Always Saved," the "Prosperity Gospel," and the timing of various eschatological events.

Yet we are nevertheless the body of Christ, and we can move forward without drawing lines in the sand and taking our firing pins off safety.

Title:

// SCRIPTURE

// OBSERVATION

// APPLICATION

// PRAYER

Title:

//SCRIPTURE

//OBSERVATION

//APPLICATION

//PRAYER

Title:

//SCRIPTURE

//OBSERVATION

//APPLICATION

//PRAYER

Title:

// SCRIPTURE

// OBSERVATION

// APPLICATION

// PRAYER

Title:

// SCRIPTURE

// OBSERVATION

// APPLICATION

// PRAYER

Title:

// SCRIPTURE

// OBSERVATION

// APPLICATION

// PRAYER

Title:

// SCRIPTURE

// OBSERVATION

// APPLICATION

// PRAYER

Title:

// SCRIPTURE

// OBSERVATION

// APPLICATION

// PRAYER

Title:

// SCRIPTURE

// OBSERVATION

// APPLICATION

// PRAYER

Title:

// SCRIPTURE

// OBSERVATION

// APPLICATION

// PRAYER

Endnotes

DEDICATION
1. See Jeremiah 2:13.

INTRODUCTION
1. See 1 Samuel 30.
2. Romans 15:4.
3. See Hebrews 11:4.

CHAPTER 1
1. Proverbs 4:23 NIV.
2. Proverbs 24:32.
3. Jeremiah 17:15.
4. Jeremiah 17:16; italics indicate emphasis added, throughout.
5. Psalm 11:3.
6. Luke 10:40 NLT.
7. Luke 10:42 NASB, 1971 edition.
8. 1 Timothy 4:8 NLT.
9. Proverbs 4:23.

CHAPTER 2
1. Psalm 119:24.
2. Psalm 119:67, 71.
3. Proverbs 22:3 NLT.
4. Psalm 19:7.
5. 2 Corinthians 7:8–10 NIV.
6. 1 Corinthians 10:10–11.
7. James 3:15–16.
8. James 3:17.
9. Psalm 119:98–99.

CHAPTER 3

1. Jeremiah 15:16.
2. Luke 10:41–42.
3. John 14:16–17.
4. John 16:13.
5. Psalm 138:2 NIV.
6. 2 Timothy 3:7.
7. Hebrews 11:4.
8. James 1:9 NASB 1971.
9. Proverbs 24:30–32.
10. Romans 15:4 NIV.
11. Galatians 4:1–2.
12. Proverbs 13:20.
13. Hebrews 11:39–40.

CHAPTER 4

1. Psalm 34:8.
2. 1 Kings 4:29 NIV.
3. Proverbs 9:10; cf. Psalm 111:10; Proverbs 1:7 (Here wisdom is knowledge.)
4. Ecclesiastes 4:13.
5. Joshua 1:8.
6. John 15:1–5.
7. John 15:7, 3.
8. John 10:4–5 NIV.
9. 2 Corinthians 11:14–15 NIV.
10. Matthew 24:24 NIV; cf. Mark 13:22.
11. James 1:5–6 NLT.
12. Isaiah 55:9.
13. Psalm 32:8 NIV.

CHAPTER 5

1. Luke 10:41–42 NLT.
2. John 6:63.
3. Philippians 3:10–11.
4. Philippians 3:13–14 NIV.
5. Luke 22:39.
6. Luke 5:16 NIV.

7. Genesis 5:23–24 NIV.
8. Hebrews 11:5 NIV.
9. See Ephesians 6:10–17.
10. Ephesians 6:17.
11. Proverbs 22:18.
12. See John 14:26.
13. See Luke 4; cf. Matthew 4.
14. Psalm 46:10 NIV.

CHAPTER 6

1. Jeremiah 30:2 NIV.
2. Isaiah 30:21.
3. 2 Timothy 3:16–17 NLT.
4. See Ephesians 1:18.
5. Jeremiah 30:2 NIV.
6. Revelation 2:11.
7. Deuteronomy 17:18–20 NLT.
8. Isaiah 30:21.
9. Proverbs 8:19.

CHAPTER 7

1. 1 Corinthians 8:2 THE MESSAGE.
2. Jeremiah 17:16.
3. Proverbs 25:11 NIV.
4. Mark 12:30; cf. Matthew 22:37; Luke 10:27.
5. Psalm 37:37 NIV.
6. Luke 12:27 NIV.
7. Galatians 3:6–7 NIV.
8. Mark 12:41–42.
9. John 8:37.
10. 1 Corinthians 8:1–2 NIV.
11. James 1:23–25 NIV.
12. John 13:17.
13. Psalm 1:1–3.
14. Matthew 25:28.

CHAPTER 8

1. John 6:35 NIV.
2. Jeremiah 15:16.

3. Psalm 78:25.
4. Exodus 16:4 NIV.
5. Exodus 16:20 NIV.
6. Luke 11:3 NIV.
7. Hebrews 2:1 NIV.
8. Proverbs 8:34 NIV.
9. Romans 10:17.
10. Matthew 23:2–3 NIV.
11. Amos 8:11.

CHAPTER 9

1. Jeremiah 17:7–8 NIV.
2. Psalm 46:10 NIV.
3. James 1:25.
4. Isaiah 45:19 NIV.
5. Jeremiah 29:13–14 NIV.
6. Mark 12:30.
7. John 8:32 NIV.
8. 1 John 5:3 NLT.
9. Mark 6:3.
10. Mark 6:5.
11. Psalm 119:165 KJV.
12. Isaiah 42:4.
13. Psalm 42:1.
14. 2 Kings 5:13, paraphrased.
15. Hebrews 4:13.
16. Psalm 139:23–24.
17. Psalm 119:9, 11.
18. Genesis 20:3.
19. Genesis 20:5.
20. Genesis 20:6.
21. Genesis 20:7.
22. Genesis 20:18.
23. 2 Peter 3:9 NIV.

CHAPTER 10

1. Deuteronomy 17:18–19 NLT.
2. Proverbs 27:17.

3. Amos 8:11.
4. Robert Lewis, Wayne Cordeiro, and Warren Bird, *Culture Shift: Transforming Your Church From the Inside Out* (San Francisco: Jossey-Bass, 2005).
5. *Life Journal* (Oregon: Life Journal Resources).

CHAPTER 11
1. Jeremiah 15:16.
2. Jeremiah 23:29 NIV.
3. 2 Corinthians 10:3–5 NIV.
4. 2 Peter 1:20–21.
5. 2 Timothy 3:16–17.
6. Psalm 22:1; cf. Matthew 27:46; Mark 15:34.
7. Revelation 1:1–3 NIV.
8. Isaiah 40:8.
9. Psalm 119:89 NIV.
10. Matthew 5:18.
11. Mark 12:24.
12. 1 Timothy 4:1.
13. Jeremiah 15:19.
14. Acts 4:13.
15. Luke 6:40 NIV.
16. 1 Corinthians 15:33.
17. Isaiah 50:4.

CHAPTER 12
1. John 6:45 NIV.
2. Ruth 3:10 NIV.
3. 1 Corinthians 2:16.
4. Acts 4:13 NIV.
5. F. Kefa Sempangi, *A Distant Grief: The Real Story Behind the Martyrdom of Christians in Uganda* (Eugene, OR: Wipf and Stock, 2005).
6. 1 Chronicles 11:17 NIV.

A FINAL WORD
1. Exodus 33:16 NIV.
2. Ezra 7:6.
3. Ezra 7:28.

4. See Exodus 13:21.
5. Exodus 33:15–16.
6. Ecclesiastes 1:2; cf. 12:8.
7. Exodus 33:12–14 NIV.
8. John 14:16.
9. Jeremiah 29:11.
10. Genesis 1:1–2.
11. Ephesians 2:10.
12. Psalm 39:5.
13. James 4:14.
14. Exodus 33:15–16 NIV.

APPENDIX

1. 2 Kings 6:17.
2. 2 Peter 3:15–16 NLT.
3. Psalm 119:18.
4. 1 Chronicles 21:24.
5. Galatians 6:1.

About the Author

WAYNE CORDEIRO is senior pastor of New Hope Christian Fellowship in Honolulu, Hawaii, one of the nation's fastest-growing churches. Pioneered by him, it has grown to over 12,000 in weekend attendance with over 34,000 making a first-time decision for Christ since 1995. Wayne is an author, songwriter, and highly sought after conference speaker. His books include *Doing Church As a Team, Attitudes That Attract Success,* and *The Dream Releasers.* He is a church planter at heart and has helped to plant 93 churches in the USA and the Pacific Rim. Wayne and his wife, Anna, have three children and live in Honolulu.

For more information go to *www.divinementor.com.*

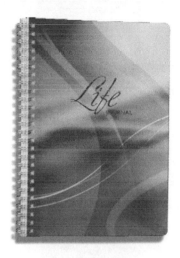

Life Journals

Capture God's promises
as well as the counsel of
divine mentors as you
meet with them in your
daily devotions.

MORE OF THE BEST FROM WAYNE CORDEIRO

Doing Church As A Team
The Miracle of Teamwork and
How It Transforms Churches

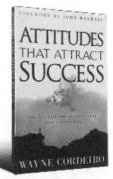

Attitudes That Attract Success
You're Only One Attitude Away
from a GREAT Life!

Culture Shift
Transforming Your Church
from the Inside Out

The Dream Releasers
How to Help Others Realize Their
Dreams While Achieving Your Own

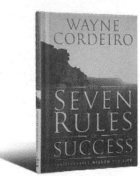

The Seven Rules of Success
Indispensible Wisdom for Life